D1488418

THE VARIORUM AND DEFINITIVE EDITION
OF THE POETICAL AND PROSE WRITINGS OF

EDWARD FITZGERALD

THE VARIORUM AND DEFINITIVE EDITION
OF THE POETICAL AND PROSE WRITINGS OF
EDWARD FITZGERALD,
INCLUDING A COMPLETE BIBLIOGRAPHY AND
INTERESTING PERSONAL AND LITERARY NOTES
THE WHOLE COLLECTED AND ARRANGED BY
GEORGE BENTHAM
AND WITH AN INTRODUCTION BY
EDMUND GOSSE

VOLUME THREE

PHAETON PRESS
NEW YORK   MCMLXVII

Originally Published 1902
Reprinted 1967

Library of Congress Catalog Card Number 67-18645

Printed in U.S.A.
EDWARDS BROTHERS, INC.
Ann Arbor, Michigan

CONTENTS.

PAGE

RUBÁIYÁT OF OMAR KHAYYÁM, FIFTH EDITION   1

TITLE-PAGE OF RUBÁIYÁT OF OMAR KHAYYÁM, THIRD EDITION 3

EXTRACTS FROM FITZGERALD'S LETTERS RELATING TO "SALÁMÁN AND ABSÁL," THIRD EDITION ix

SALÁMÁN AND ABSÁL, FOURTH EDITION . . . 41

EXTRACTS FROM FITZGERALD'S LETTERS RELATING TO "EUPHRANOR," THIRD EDITION . . xi

"EUPHRANOR," THIRD EDITION 109

EXTRACTS FROM FITZGERALD'S LETTERS RELATING TO "AGAMEMNON," SECOND EDITION . . xv

AGAMEMNON, THIRD EDITION 193

(NOTE. The original pagination of the works is indicated by italic numerals in parentheses in the margins, and the various title-pages are reproduced in facsimile.)

RUBÁIYÁT
OF
OMAR KHAYYÁM

Welcome, Prince of Horsemen, welcome!
Ride afield, and strike the Ball!

RUBÁIYÁT

OF

OMAR KHAYYÁM,

THE ASTRONOMER-POET OF PERSIA.

Rendered into English Verse.

THIRD EDITION.

LONDON:

BERNARD QUARITCH,

PICCADILLY.

1872.

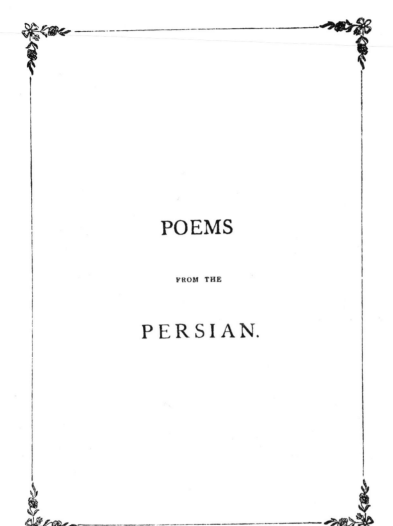

POEMS

FROM THE

PERSIAN.

RUBÁIYÁT

OF

OMAR KHAYYÁM;

AND THE

SALÁMÁN AND ÁBSÁL

OF

JÁMÍ;

RENDERED INTO ENGLISH VERSE.

BERNARD QUARITCH; 15 PICCADILLY, LONDON.

1879.

RUBÁIYÁT

OF

OMAR KHAYYÁM,

THE ASTRONOMER-POET OF PERSIA.

Rendered into English Verse.

FOURTH EDITION.

OMAR KHAYYÁM,
THE
ASTRONOMER-POET OF PERSIA.

[The biography of Omar Khayyám prefixed to the third edition of
the "Rubáiyát" (1873) and to the posthumous edition (1889) are
the same as that printed in the second edition (1868)—save that
the anecdote quoted from Nicolas * is omitted, and the following
paragraph is substituted for the final one]—

However, as there is some traditional presumption, and
certainly the opinion of some learned men, in favour of
Omar's being a Súfí—and even something of a Saint—
those who please may so interpret his Wine and Cup-
bearer. On the other hand, as there is far more historical
certainty of his being a Philosopher, of scientific Insight
and Ability far beyond that of the Age and Country he
lived in; of such moderate worldly Ambition as becomes
a Philosopher, and such moderate wants as rarely satisfy
a Debauchee; other readers may be content to believe with
me that, while the Wine Omar celebrates is simply the
Juice of the Grape, he bragged more than he drank of it,
in very defiance perhaps of that Spiritual Wine which
left its Votaries sunk in Hypocrisy or Disgust.

* Vol. II. p. 16–17.

RUBÁIYÁT

OF

OMAR KHAYYÁM OF NAISHÁPÚR.

I WAKE! For the Sun, who scatter'd into flight
  The Stars before him from the Field of Night,
    Drives Night along with them from Heav'n, and strikes
  The Sultán's Turret with a Shaft of Light.

II Before the phantom of False morning died,
  Methought a Voice within the Tavern cried,
    "When all the Temple is prepared within,
  "Why nods the drowsy Worshipper outside?"

III And, as the Cock crew, those who stood before
  The Tavern shouted—"Open then the Door!
    "You know how little while we have to stay,
  "And, once departed, may return no more."

IV Now the New Year reviving old Desires,   (2)
  The thoughtful Soul to Solitude retires,
    Where the WHITE HAND OF MOSES on the Bough
  Puts out, and Jesus from the Ground suspires.

v Iram indeed is gone with all his Rose,
   And Jamshyd's Sev'n-ring'd Cup where no one knows;
   But still a Ruby kindles in the Vine,*
   And many a Garden by the Water blows.

vi And David's lips are lockt; but in divine
    High-piping Pehleví, with "Wine! Wine! Wine!
    "Red Wine!"—the Nightingale cries to the Rose
    That sallow cheek of hers to' incarnadine.

vii Come, fill the Cup, and in the fire of Spring
     Your Winter-garment of Repentance fling:
     The Bird of Time has but a little way
     To flutter—and the Bird is on the Wing.

viii Whether at Naishápúr or Babylon,   (3)
      Whether the Cup with sweet or bitter run,
      The Wine of Life keeps oozing drop by drop,
      The Leaves of Life keep falling one by one.

ix Each Morn a thousand Roses brings, you say;
    Yes, but where leaves the Rose of Yesterday?
    And this first Summer month that brings the Rose
    Shall take Jamshyd and Kaikobád away.

* But still a Ruby gushes from the Vine. (Third edition.)

x Well, let it take them! What have we to do
With Kaikobád the Great, or Kaikhosrú?
    Let Zál and Rustum bluster as they will,*
Or Hátim call to Supper—heed not you.

xi With me along the strip of Herbage strown
That just divides the desert from the sown,
    Where name of Slave and Sultán is forgot—
And Peace to Mahmúd on his golden Throne!

xii A Book of Verses underneath the Bough,   (4)
A Jug of Wine, a Loaf of Bread—and Thou
    Beside me singing in the Wilderness—
Oh, Wilderness were Paradise enow!

xiii Some for the Glories of This World; and some
Sigh for the Prophet's Paradise to come;
    Ah, take the Cash, and let the Credit go,
Nor heed the rumble of a distant Drum!

xiv Look to the blowing Rose about us—"Lo,
"Laughing," she says, "into the world I blow,
    "At once the silken tassel of my Purse
"Tear, and its Treasure on the Garden throw."

* Let Zál and Rustum thunder as they will. (Third edition.)

[15]

xv And those who husbanded the Golden Grain,
And those who flung it to the winds like Rain,
Alike to no such aureate Earth are turn'd
As, buried once, Men want dug up again.

xvi The Worldly Hope men set their Hearts upon   (5)
Turns Ashes—or it prospers; and anon,
Like Snow upon the Desert's dusty Face,
Lighting a little hour or two—is gone.*

xvii Think, in this batter'd Caravanserai
Whose Portals are alternate Night and Day,
How Sultán after Sultán with his Pomp
Abode his destined Hour, and went his way.

xviii They say the Lion and the Lizard keep
The Courts where Jamshyd gloried and drank deep:
And Bahrám, that great Hunter—the Wild Ass
Stamps o'er his Head, but cannot break his Sleep.

xix I sometimes think that never blows so red
The Rose as where some buried Cæsar bled;
That every Hyacinth the Garden wears
Dropt in her Lap from some once lovely Head.

* Lighting a little hour or two—was gone. (Third and Fourth
editions.)

xx And this reviving Herb whose tender Green   *(6)*
    Fledges the River-Lip on which we lean—
      Ah, lean upon it lightly! for who knows
    From what once lovely Lip it springs unseen!

xxi Ah, my Belovéd, fill the Cup that clears
    To-day of past Regrets and future Fears:
      To-morrow!—why, To-morrow I may be
    Myself with Yesterday's Sev'n thousand Years.

xxii For some we loved, the loveliest and the best
    That from his Vintage rolling Time hath prest,
      Have drunk their Cup a Round or two before,
    And one by one crept silently to rest.

xxiii And we, that now make merry in the Room
    They left, and Summer dresses in new bloom,
      Ourselves must we beneath the Couch of Earth
    Descend—ourselves to make a Couch—for whom?

xxiv Ah, make the most of what we yet may spend,   *(7)*
    Before we too into the Dust descend;
      Dust into Dust, and under Dust to lie,
    Sans Wine, sans Song, sans Singer, and—sans End!

xxv Alike for those who for To-DAY prepare,
And those that after some To-MORROW stare,
A Muezzín from the Tower of Darkness cries,
"Fools! your Reward is neither Here nor There."

xxvi Why all the Saints and Sages who discuss'd
Of the Two Worlds so wisely—they are thrust *
Like foolish Prophets forth; their Words to Scorn
Are scatter'd, and their Mouths are stopt with Dust.

xxvii Myself when young did eagerly frequent
Doctor and Saint, and heard great argument
About it and about: but evermore
Came out by the same door where in I went.

xxviii With them the seed of Wisdom did I sow,   (8)
And with mine own hand wrought to make it grow;
And this was all the Harvest that I reap'd—
"I came like Water, and like Wind I go."

xxix Into this Universe, and *Why* not knowing
Nor *Whence*, like Water willy-nilly flowing;
And out of it, as Wind along the Waste,
I know not *Whither*, willy-nilly blowing.

* Of the Two Worlds so learnedly are thrust. (Third edition.)

xxx What, without asking, hither hurried *Whence?*
And, without asking, *Whither* hurried hence!
  Oh, many a Cup of this forbidden Wine
Must drown the memory of that insolence!

xxxi Up from Earth's Centre through the Seventh Gate
I rose, and on the Throne of Saturn sate,
  And many a Knot unravell'd by the Road;
But not the Master-knot of Human Fate.

xxxii There was the Door to which I found no Key;   (9)
There was the Veil through which I might not see: *
  Some little talk awhile of ME and THEE
There was—and then no more of THEE and ME.

xxxiii Earth could not answer; nor the Seas that mourn
In flowing Purple, of their Lord forlorn;
  Nor rolling Heaven, with all his Signs reveal'd
And hidden by the sleeve of Night and Morn.

xxxiv Then of the THEE IN ME who works behind
The Veil, I lifted up my hands to find
  A lamp amid the Darkness; and I heard,
As from Without—"THE ME WITHIN THEE BLIND!"

* There was the Veil through which I could not see.   (Third edition.)

[19]

xxxv Then to the Lip of this poor earthen Urn
I lean'd, the Secret of my Life to learn:
    And Lip to Lip it murmur'd—"While you live,
"Drink!—for, once dead, you never shall return."

xxxvi I think the Vessel, that with fugitive   (10)
Articulation answer'd, once did live,
    And drink; and Ah! the passive Lip I kiss'd,
How many Kisses might it take—and give!

xxxvii For I remember stopping by the way
To watch a Potter thumping his wet Clay:
    And with its all-obliterated Tongue
It murmur'd—"Gently, Brother, gently, pray!"

xxxviii* And has not such a Story from of Old
Down Man's successive generations roll'd
    Of such a clod of saturated Earth
Cast by the Maker into Human mould?

xxxix And not a drop that from our Cups we throw
For Earth to drink of, but may steal below
    To quench the fire of Anguish in some Eye
There hidden—far beneath, and long ago.

* xxxviii Listen—a moment listen!—Of the same
Poor Earth from which that Human Whisper came
  The luckless Mould in which Mankind was cast
They did compose, and call'd him by the name. (Third
edition.)

xl As then the Tulip for her morning sup (11)
　　Of Heav'nly Vintage from the soil looks up,
　　　　Do you devoutly do the like, till Heav'n
　　To Earth invert you—like an empty Cup.

xli Perplext no more with Human or Divine,
　　To-morrow's tangle to the winds resign,
　　　　And lose your fingers in the tresses of
　　The Cypress-slender Minister of Wine.

xlii And if the Wine you drink, the Lip you press,
　　End in what All begins and ends in—Yes;
　　　　Think that you are TO-DAY what YESTERDAY
　　You were—To-MORROW you shall not be less.

xliii So when that Angel of the darker Drink *
　　At last shall find you by the river-brink,
　　　　And, offering his Cup, invite your Soul
　　Forth to your Lips to quaff—you shall not shrink.

xliv Why, if the Soul can fling the Dust aside, (12)
　　And naked on the Air of Heaven ride,
　　　　Were 't not a Shame—were 't not a Shame for him
　　In this clay carcase crippled to abide?

* So when the Angel of the darker Drink. (Third and Fourth
editions.)

XLV   'T is but a Tent where takes his one day's rest
A Sultán to the realm of Death addrest;
    The Sultán rises, and the dark Ferrásh
Strikes, and prepares it for another Guest.

XLVI   And fear not lest Existence closing your
Account, and mine, should know the like no more;
    The Eternal Sákí from that Bowl has pour'd
Millions of Bubbles like us, and will pour.

XLVII   When You and I behind the Veil are past,
Oh, but the long, long while the World shall last,
    Which of our Coming and Departure heeds
As the Sea's self should heed a pebble-cast.*

XLVIII   A Moment's Halt—a momentary taste   *(13)*
Of BEING from the Well amid the Waste—
    And Lo!—the phantom Caravan has reach'd
The NOTHING it set out from—Oh, make haste!

XLIX   Would you that spangle of Existence spend
About THE SECRET—quick about it, Friend!
    A Hair perhaps divides the False and True—
And upon what, prithee, may life depend?†

* As the Sev'n Seas should heed a pebble-cast. (Third edition.)
† And upon what, prithee, does Life depend? (Third and Fourth editions.)

L A Hair perhaps divides the False and True;
 Yes; and a single Alif were the clue—
  Could you but find it—to the Treasure-house,
And peradventure to THE MASTER too;

LI Whose secret Presence, through Creation's veins
 Running Quicksilver-like eludes your pains;
  Taking all shapes from Máh to Máhi; and
They change and perish all—but He remains;

LII A moment guess'd—then back behind the Fold   *(14)*
 Immerst of Darkness round the Drama roll'd
  Which, for the Pastime of Eternity,
He doth Himself contrive, enact, behold.

LIII But if in vain, down on the stubborn floor
 Of Earth, and up to Heav'n's unopening Door,
  You gaze TO-DAY, while You are You—how then
TO-MORROW, You when shall be You no more?

LIV Waste not your Hour, nor in the vain pursuit
 Of This and That endeavour and dispute;
  Better be jocund with the fruitful Grape
That sadden after none, or bitter, Fruit.

[23]

LV You know, my Friends, with what a brave Carouse
I made a Second Marriage in my house;
Divorced old barren Reason from my Bed,
And took the Daughter of the Vine to Spouse.

LVI For "Is" and "Is-NOT" though with Rule and Line, (15)
And "UP-AND-DOWN" by Logic I define,
Of all that one should care to fathom, I
Was never deep in anything but—Wine.

LVII Ah, but my Computations, People say,
Reduced the Year to better reckoning?—Nay,
'Twas only striking from the Calendar
Unborn To-morrow, and dead Yesterday.

LVIII And lately, by the Tavern Door agape,
Came shining through the Dusk an Angel Shape
Bearing a Vessel on his Shoulder; and
He bid me taste of it; and 't was—the Grape!

LIX The Grape that can with Logic absolute
The Two-and-Seventy jarring Sects confute:
The sovereign Alchemist that in a trice
Life's leaden metal into Gold transmute:

LX The mighty Mahmúd, Allah-breathing Lord,   *(16)*
    That all the misbelieving and black Horde
        Of Fears and Sorrows that infest the Soul
    Scatters before him with his whirlwind Sword.

LXI Why, be this Juice the growth of God, who dare
    Blaspheme the twisted tendril as a Snare?
        A Blessing, we should use it, should we not?
    And if a Curse—why, then, Who set it there?

LXII I must abjure the Balm of Life, I must,
    Scared by some After-reckoning ta'en on trust,
        Or lured with Hope of some Diviner Drink,
    To fill the Cup—when crumbled into Dust!

LXIII Oh threats of Hell and Hopes of Paradise!
    One thing at least is certain—*This* Life flies;
        One thing is certain and the rest is Lies;
    The Flower that once has blown for ever dies.

LXIV Strange, is it not? that of the myriads who   *(17)*
    Before us pass'd the door of Darkness through
        Not one returns to tell us of the Road,
    Which to discover we must travel too.

LXV The Revelations of Devout and Learn'd
Who rose before us, and as Prophets burn'd,
Are all but Stories, which, awoke from Sleep
They told their comrades, and to Sleep return'd.*

LXVI I sent my Soul through the Invisible,
Some letter of that After-life to spell:
And by and by my Soul return'd to me,
And answer'd "I Myself am Heav'n and Hell:"

LXVII Heav'n but the Vision of fulfill'd Desire,
And Hell the Shadow from a Soul on fire,†
Cast on the Darkness into which Ourselves,
So late emerged from, shall so soon expire.

LXVIII We are no other than a moving row   *(18)*
Of Magic Shadow-shapes that come and go
Round with the Sun-illumined Lantern held ‡
In Midnight by the Master of the Show;

LXIX But helpless Pieces of the Game He plays§
Upon this Chequer-board of Nights and Days;
Hither and thither moves, and checks, and slays,
And one by one back in the Closet lays.

* They told their fellows, and to Sleep return'd. (Third edition.)
† And Hell the Shadow of a Soul on fire. (Third edition.)
‡ Round with this Sun-illumin'd Lantern held. (Third edition.)
§ Impotent Pieces of the Game He plays. (Third edition.)

LXX The Ball no question makes of Ayes and Noes,
But Here or There as strikes the Player goes; *
And He that toss'd you down into the Field,
He knows about it all—HE knows—HE knows!

LXXI The Moving Finger writes; and, having writ,
Moves on: nor all your Piety nor Wit
Shall lure it back to cancel half a Line,
Nor all your Tears wash out a Word of it.

LXXII And that inverted Bowl they call the Sky, (*19*)
Whereunder crawling coop'd we live and die,
Lift not your hands to *It* for help—for It
As impotently moves as you or I.†

LXXIII With Earth's first Clay They did the Last Man knead,
And there of the Last Harvest sow'd the Seed:
And the first Morning of Creation wrote
What the Last Dawn of Reckoning shall read.

LXXIV YESTERDAY *This* Day's Madness did prepare;
To-MORROW's Silence, Triumph, or Despair:
Drink! for you know not whence you came, nor why:
Drink! for you know not why you go, nor where.

* But Right or Left as strikes the Player goes. (Third edition.)
† As impotently rolls as you or I. (Third edition.)

LXXV I tell you this—When, started from the Goal,
Over the flaming shoulders of the Foal
Of Heav'n Parwín and Mushtarí they flung,
In my predestined Plot of Dust and Soul

LXXVI The Vine had struck a fibre: which about   (20)
If clings my Being—let the Dervish flout;
Of my Base metal may be filed a Key,
That shall unlock the Door he howls without.

LXXVII And this I know: whether the one True Light
Kindle to Love, or Wrath-consume me quite,
One Flash of It within the Tavern caught
Better than in the Temple lost outright.

LXXVIII What! out of senseless Nothing to provoke
A conscious Something to resent the yoke
Of unpermitted Pleasure, under pain
Of Everlasting Penalties, if broke!

LXXIX What! from his helpless Creature be repaid
Pure Gold for what he lent him dross-allay'd—*
Sue for a Debt he never did contract,†
And cannot answer—Oh the sorry trade!

* Pure Gold for what he lent us dross-allay'd. (Third edition.)
† Sue for a Debt we never did contract. (Third and Fourth editions.)

[28]

LXXX Oh Thou, who didst with pitfall and with gin *(21)*
Beset the Road I was to wander in,
  Thou wilt not with Predestined Evil round
Enmesh, and then impute my Fall to Sin!

LXXXI Oh Thou, who Man of baser Earth didst make,
And ev'n with Paradise devise the Snake:
  For all the Sin wherewith the Face of Man
Is blacken'd—Man's forgiveness give—and take!

.   .   .   .

LXXXII As under cover of departing Day
Slunk hunger-stricken Ramazán away,
  Once more within the Potter's house alone
I stood, surrounded by the Shapes of Clay.

LXXXIII Shapes of all Sorts and Sizes, great and small, *(22)*
That stood along the floor and by the wall;
  And some loquacious Vessels were; and some
Listen'd perhaps, but never talk'd at all.

LXXXIV Said one among them—"Surely not in vain
"My substance of the common Earth was ta'en
  "And to this Figure moulded, to be broke,
Or trampled back to shapeless Earth again."

LXXXV Then said a Second—"Ne'er a peevish Boy
"Would break the Bowl from which he drank in joy;
"And He that with his hand the Vessel made
Will surely not in after Wrath destroy."

LXXXVI After a momentary silence spake
Some Vessel of a more ungainly Make;
"They sneer at me for leaning all awry:
"What! did the Hand then of the Potter shake?"

LXXXVII Whereat some one of the loquacious Lot— (23)
I think a Súfi pipkin—waxing hot—
"All this of Pot and Potter—Tell me then,
"Who is the Potter, pray, and who the Pot?" *

LXXXVIII "Why," said another, "Some there are who tell
"Of one who threatens he will toss to Hell
"The luckless Pots he marr'd in making—Pish!
"He 's a Good Fellow, and 't will all be well."

LXXXIX "Well," murmur'd one, "Let whoso make or buy,
"My Clay with long Oblivion is gone dry:
"But fill me with the old familiar Juice,
"Methinks I might recover by and by."

* " Who makes—Who sells—Who buys—Who *is* the Pot?" (Third
edition.)

xc So while the Vessels one by one were speaking,
    The little Moon look'd in that all were seeking:
        And then they jogg'd each other, "Brother! Bro-
        ther!
    "Now for the Porter's shoulder-knot a-creaking."

(24)

.   .   .   .

xci Ah, with the Grape my fading Life provide,
    And wash the Body whence the Life has died,
        And lay me, shrouded in the living Leaf,
    By some not unfrequented Garden-side.

xcii That ev'n my buried Ashes such a snare
     Of Vintage shall fling up into the Air
        As not a True-believer passing by
     But shall be overtaken unaware.

xciii Indeed the Idols I have loved so long
      Have done my credit in this World much wrong:*
          Have drown'd my Glory in a shallow Cup,
      And sold my Reputation for a Song.

* Have done my credit in Men's eye much wrong. (Third edition.)

[31]

xciv Indeed, indeed, Repentance oft before   *(25)*
　　　I swore—but was I sober when I swore?
　　　　　And then and then came Spring, and Rose-in-hand
　　　My thread-bare Penitence apieces tore.

xcv And much as Wine has play'd the Infidel,
　　　And robb'd me of my Robe of Honour—Well,
　　　　　I wonder often what the Vintners buy
　　　One half so precious as the stuff they sell.

xcvi Yet Ah, that Spring should vanish with the Rose!
　　　That Youth's sweet-scented manuscript should close!
　　　　　The Nightingale that in the branches sang,
　　　Ah whence, and whither flown again, who knows!

xcvii Would but the Desert of the Fountain yield
　　　One glimpse—if dimly, yet indeed, reveal'd,
　　　　　To which the fainting Traveller might spring,
　　　As springs the trampled herbage of the field!

xcviii Would but some wingéd Angel ere too late   *(26)*
　　　Arrest the yet unfolded Roll of Fate,
　　　　　And make the stern Recorder otherwise
　　　Enregister, or quite obliterate!

XCIX Ah Love! could you and I with Him conspire
     To grasp this sorry Scheme of Things entire,
         Would we not shatter it to bits—and then
     Re-mould it nearer to the Heart's Desire!

     .   .   .   .

  C Yon rising Moon that looks for us again—
     How oft hereafter will she wax and wane;
         How oft hereafter rising look for us
     Through this same Garden—and for *one* in vain!

 CI And when like her, oh Sákí, you shall pass   *(27)*
     Among the Guests Star-scatter'd on the Grass,
         And in your joyous errand reach the spot *
     Where I made One—turn down an empty Glass!

* And in your blissful errand reach the spot. (Third edition.)

                    TAMÁM.

NOTES.

(Stanza II.) The *"False Dawn;" Subhi Kázib,* a transient Light on the Horizon about an hour before the *Subhi sádik,* or True Dawn; a well-known Phenomenon in the East.

(IV.) New Year. Beginning with the Vernal Equinox, it must be remembered; and (howsoever the old Solar Year is practically superseded by the clumsy *Lunar* Year that dates from the Mohammedan Hijra) still commemorated by a Festival that is said to have been appointed by the very Jamshyd whom Omar so often talks of, and whose yearly Calendar he helped to rectify.

"The sudden approach and rapid advance of the Spring," says Mr. Binning,[1] "are very striking. Before the Snow is well off the Ground, the Trees burst into Blossom, and the Flowers start forth from the Soil. At *Naw Rooz* (*their* New Year's Day) the Snow was lying in patches on the Hills and in the shaded Vallies, while the Fruit-trees in the Gardens were budding beautifully, and green Plants and Flowers springing up on the Plains on every side—

'And on old Hyems' Chin and icy Crown
'An odorous Chaplet of sweet Summer buds
'Is, as in mockery, set.——'

Among the Plants newly appeared I recognised some old Acquaintances I had not seen for many a Year: among these, two varieties of the Thistle—a coarse species of Daisy, like the 'Horse-gowan' —red and white Clover—the Dock—the blue Corn-flower—and that vulgar Herb the Dandelion rearing its | yellow crest on the Banks of *(29)* the Watercourses." The Nightingale was not yet heard, for the Rose was not yet blown: but an almost identical Blackbird and Woodpecker helped to make up something of a North-country Spring.

"The White Hand of Moses." Exodus iv. 6; where Moses draws forth his Hand—not, according to the Persians, *"leprous as Snow,"* —but *white,* as our May-blossom in Spring perhaps. According to them also the Healing Power of Jesus resided in his Breath.

(V.) Iram, planted by King Shaddád, and now sunk somewhere in the Sands of Arabia. Jamshyd's Seven-ring'd Cup was typical of the 7 Heavens, 7 Planets, 7 Seas, &c., and was a *Divining Cup.*

(VI.) *Péhlevi,* the old Heroic *Sanskrit* of Persia. Háfiz also speaks of the Nightingale's *Péhlevi,* which did not change with the People's.

I am not sure if the fourth line refers to the Red Rose looking sickly, or to the Yellow Rose that ought to be Red; Red, White, and

[1] Two Years' Travel in Persia, &c., I. 165.

Yellow Roses all common in Persia. I think that Southey, in his
Common-Place Book, quotes from some Spanish author about the
Rose being White till 10 o'clock; "Rosa perfecta" at 2; and "perfecta
incarnada" at 5.

(x.) Rustum, the "Hercules" of Persia, and Zál his Father, whose
exploits are among the most celebrated in the Sháh-náma. Hátim
Tai a well-known type of Oriental Generosity.

(xiii.) A Drum—beaten outside a Palace.

(xiv.) That is, the Rose's Golden Centre.

(xviii.) Persepolis: called also *Takht-i-Jamshyd*—THE THRONE OF
JAMSHYD, "*King-Splendid*," of the mythical *Peshdádian* Dynasty,
and supposed (according to the Sháh-náma) to have been founded
(30) and built by him. Others refer it to the Work of|the Genie King,
Ján Ibn Ján—who also built the Pyramids—before the time of Adam.

BAHRÁM GÚR—*Bahrám of the Wild Ass*—a Sassanian Sovereign—
had also his Seven Castles (like the King of Bohemia!) each of a
different Colour; each with a Royal Mistress within; each of whom
tells him a Story, as told in one of the most famous Poems of Persia, written by Amir Khusraw: all these Sevens also figuring (according to Eastern Mysticism) the Seven Heavens; and perhaps the Book
itself that Eighth, into which the mystical Seven transcend, and
within which they revolve. The Ruins of Three of those Towers are
yet shown by the Peasantry; as also the Swamp in which Bahrám
sunk, like the Master of Ravenswood, while pursuing his *Gúr*.

> The Palace that to Heav'n his pillars threw,
> And Kings the forehead on his threshold drew—
> I saw the solitary Ringdove there,
> And "Coo, coo, coo," she cried; and "Coo, coo, coo."

This Quatrain Mr. Binning found, among several of Háfiz and
others, inscribed by some stray hand among the ruins of Persepolis.
The Ringdove's ancient *Péhlevi, Coo, Coo, Coo*, signifies also in Persian "*Where? Where? Where?*" In Attár's "Bird-parliament" she
is reproved by the Leader of the Birds for sitting still, and for ever
harping on that one note of lamentation for her lost Yúsuf.

Apropos of Omar's Red Roses in Stanza xix, I am reminded of an
old English Superstition, that our Anemone Pulsatilla, or purple
"Pasque Flower" (which grows plentifully about the Fleam Dyke,
near Cambridge), grows only where Danish Blood has been spilt.

(xxi.) A thousand years to each Planet.

(xxxi.) Saturn, Lord of the Seventh Heaven.

(31) (xxxii.) ME-AND-THEE: some dividual Existence or Personality distinct from the Whole.

(xxxvii.) One of the Persian Poets—Attár, I think—has a pretty
story about this. A thirsty Traveller dips his hand into a Spring of
Water to drink from. By-and-by comes another who draws up and

drinks from an earthen Bowl, and then departs, leaving his Bowl behind him. The first Traveller takes it up for another draught; but is surprised to find that the same Water which had tasted sweet from his own hand tastes bitter from the earthen Bowl. But a Voice—from Heaven, I think—tells him the clay from which the Bowl is made was once *Man;* and, into whatever shape renewed, can never lose the bitter flavour of Mortality.

(XXXIX.) The custom of throwing a little Wine on the ground before drinking still continues in Persia, and perhaps generally in the East. Mons. Nicolas considers it "un signe de libéralité, et en même temps un avertissement que le buveur doit vider sa coupe jusqu'à la dernière goutte." Is it not more likely an ancient Superstition; a Libation to propitiate Earth, or make her an Accomplice in the illicit Revel? Or, perhaps, to divert the Jealous Eye by some sacrifice of superfluity, as with the Ancients of the West? With Omar we see something more is signified; the precious Liquor is not lost, but sinks into the ground to refresh the dust of some poor Wine-worshipper foregone.

Thus Háfiz, copying Omar in so many ways: "When thou drinkest Wine pour a draught on the ground. Wherefore fear the Sin which brings to another Gain?"

(XLIII.) According to one beautiful Oriental Legend, Azräel accomplishes his mission by holding to the nostril an Apple from the Tree of Life.

This and the two following stanzas would have been withdrawn, as *(32)* somewhat *de trop,* from the Text, but for advice which I least like to disregard.

(LI.) From Máh to Máhi; from Fish to Moon.

(LVI.) A Jest, of course, at his Studies. A curious mathematical Quatrain of Omar's has been pointed out to me; the more curious because almost exactly parallel'd by some Verses of Doctor Donne's, that are quoted in Izaak Walton's Lives! Here is Omar: "You and I are the image of a pair of compasses; though we have two heads (sc. our *feet*) we have one body; when we have fixed the centre for our circle, we bring our heads (sc. feet) together at the end." Dr. Donne:

> If we be two, we two are so
> As stiff twin-compasses are two;
> Thy Soul, the fixt foot, makes no show
> To move, but does if the other do.

> And though thine in the centre sit,
> Yet when my other far does roam,
> Thine leans and hearkens after it,
> And grows erect as mine comes home.

> Such thou must be to me, who must
> Like the other foot obliquely run;
> Thy firmness makes my circle just,
> And me to end where I begun.

NOTES.

(LIX.) The Seventy-two Religions supposed to divide the World, *including* Islamism, as some think: but others not.

(LX.) Alluding to Sultan Mahmúd's Conquest of India and its dark people.

(33) (LXVIII.) *Fánúsi khiyál*, a Magic-lantern still used in India; the cylindrical Interior being painted with various Figures, and so lightly poised and ventilated as to revolve round the lighted Candle within.

(LXX.) A very mysterious Line in the Original:

O dánad O dánad O dánad O ——

breaking off something like our Wood-pigeon's Note, which she is said to take up just where she left off.

(LXXV.) Parwín and Mushtarí—the Pleiads and Jupiter.

(LXXXVII.) This Relation of Pot and Potter to Man and his Maker figures far and wide in the Literature of the World, from the time of the Hebrew Prophets to the present; when it may finally take the name of "Pot theism," by which Mr. Carlyle ridiculed Sterling's "Pantheism." *My* Sheikh, whose knowledge flows in from all quarters, writes to me—

"Apropos of old Omar's Pots, did I ever tell you the sentence I found in 'Bishop Pearson on the Creed'? 'Thus we are wholly at the disposal of His will, and our present and future condition framed and ordered by His free, but wise and just, decrees. *Hath not the potter power over the clay, of the same lump to make one vessel unto honour, and another unto dishonour?* (Rom. ix. 21.) And can that earth-artificer have a freer power over his *brother potsherd* (both being made of the same metal), than God hath over him, who, by the strange fecundity of His omnipotent power, first made the clay out of nothing, and then him out of that?' "

And again—from a very different quarter—"I had to refer the other day to Aristophanes, and came by chance on a curious Speaking-pot story in the Vespæ, which I had quite forgotten.

(34)   Φιλοκλέων. ''Ακουε, μὴ φεῦγ'· ἐν Συβάρει γυνή ποτε
κατέαξ' ἐχῖνον.
Κατήγορος.   Ταῦτ' ἐγὼ μαρτύρομαι
Φι.   Οὐχῖνος οὖν ἔχων τιν' ἐπεμαρτύρατο·
Εἶθ' ἡ Συβαρῖτις εἶπεν, εἰ ναὶ τὰν κόραν
τὴν μαρτυρίαν ταύτην ἐάσας, ἐν τάχει
ἐπίδεσμον ἐπρίω, νοῦν ἂν εἶχες πλείονα.

"The Pot calls a bystander to be a witness to his bad treatment. The woman says, 'If, by Proserpine, instead of all this 'testifying' (comp. Cuddie and his mother in 'Old Mortality!') you would buy

yourself a rivet, it would show more sense in you!' The Scholiast
explains *echinus* as ἄγγος τι ἐκ κεράμου."

* One more illustration for the oddity's sake from the "Autobiog-
raphy of a Cornish Rector," by the late James Hamley Tregenna.
1871.

"There was one old Fellow in our Company—he was so like a
Figure in the 'Pilgrim's Progress' that Richard always called him
the 'ALLEGORY,' with a long white beard—a rare Appendage in those
days—and a Face the colour of which seemed to have been baked in,
like the Faces one used to see on Earthenware Jugs. In our Country-
dialect Earthenware is called *'Clome'*; so the Boys of the Village used
to shout out after him—'Go back to the Potter, old Clome-face, and
get baked over again.' For the 'Allegory,' though shrewd enough in
most things, had the reputation of being *'saift-baked,'* i. e. of weak
intellect." *

(xc.) At the Close of the Fasting Month, Ramazán (which makes
the Musulman unhealthy and unamiable), the first Glimpse|of the (35)
New Moon (who rules their division of the Year), is looked for with
the utmost Anxiety, and hailed with Acclamation. Then it is that the
Porter's Knot may be heard—toward the *Cellar.* Omar has elsewhere a pretty Quatrain about the same Moon—

> "Be of Good Cheer—the sullen Month will die,
> "And a young Moon requite us by and by :
> "Look how the Old one meagre, bent, and wan
> "With Age and Fast, is fainting from the Sky !"

* These two paragraphs do not appear in the Third edition. The pagination in
the margins is that of the Fourth edition.

FINIS.

EXTRACTS FROM FITZGERALD'S LETTERS RELATING TO "SALÁMÁN AND ABSÁL," THIRD EDITION.

To C. E. Norton.

Woodbridge, May 18, '79.

. . . Jámí (Salámán) is cut down to two-thirds of his former proportion, and very much improved, I think. It is still in a wrong key: Verse of Miltonic Strain, unlike the simple Eastern; I remember trying that at first but could not succeed. So there is little but the Allegory itself (not a bad one), and now condensed into a very fair Bird's Eye view; quite enough for any Allegory, I think. . . .

To E. B. Cowell.
[*June, 1879.*]

I am sorry you took time and trouble in writing me a Letter after answering my Query about the Metre. I had not seen the Shahnameh for twenty years, and made sure of its being in the same metre as Salámán: so I was obliged to have the page cancelled in which I had so said. I know not when Quaritch comes out with the two Persæ: of course, you will have a Copy sent to you. Some things in Salámán you won't like at all; but I believe that, on the whole, you will think it improved—after a while. And so, I bid Adieu to him and Omar: for I shall certainly not live to see another Edition. . . .

To W. A. Wright.

Woodbridge, Tuesday, [1879].

. . . .

Here is a Copy for you of my two Persians—I was going to say, 'If you care to have them'—but you would be obliged to say that you would care: and since you have all my Works, you shall e'en have this—if only to spew at Quaritch's Ornamentation; which leaves a pretty Book, however. Omar remains as he was; but Solomon (as Childs' men called him) is cut down about a Quarter, and all the better for it.

To H. Schütz Wilson.

[1 March, 1882.]

. . . *Jámí tells of what everybody knows, under cover of a not very skilful Allegory. I have undoubtedly improved the whole by boiling it down to about a Quarter of its original size; and there are many pretty things in it, though the blank Verse is too Miltonic for Oriental style.*

. . . .

But some six or seven years ago that Sheikh of mine, Edward Cowell, who liked the Version better than any one else, wished it to be reprinted. So I took it in hand, boiled it down to three-fourths of what it originally was, and (as you see) clapt it on the back of Omar, where I still believed it would hang somewhat of a dead weight; but that was Quaritch's look-out, not mine. I have never heard of any notice taken of it, but just now from you: and I believe that, say what you would, people would rather have the old Sinner alone. . . .

[x]

SALÁMÁN AND ABSÁL

SALÁMÁN

AND

ABSÁL.

NOTICE OF JÁMÍ'S LIFE.

Drawn from Rosenzweig's

"Biographische Notizen" of the Poet.

NÚRUDDÍN ABDURRAHMAN, Son of Maulána Nizámud-
dín Ahmed, and descended on the Mother's side from One
of the Four great " FATHERS " of Islam, was born A. H.
817, A. D. 1414, in Jám, a little Town of Khorásán,
whither his Grandfather had removed from Desht of
Ispahán and from which the Poet ultimately took his Takhallus, or Poetic name, JÁMÍ. This word also signifies
"A Cup;" wherefore, he says, " Born in Jám, and dipt in
the *"Jám "* of Holy Lore, for a double reason I must be
called JÁMÍ in the Book of Song." [1] He was celebrated
afterwards in other Oriental Titles—" Lord of Poets "
—" Elephant of Wisdom," &c., but latterly liked to call
himself " The Ancient of Herát," where he mainly resided, and eventually died.

When Five Years old he received the name of Núr-
uddín—the " Light of Faith," and even so early | began *(40)*
to show the Metal, and take the Stamp that distinguished
him through Life. In 1419, a famous Sheikh, Khwájah
Mohammed Pársá, then in the last Year of his Life, was
being carried through Jám. " I was not then Five Years

[1] *He elsewhere plays upon his name, imploring God that he may be accepted as a Cup to pass about that Spiritual Wine of which the Persian Mystical Poets make so much.*

old," says Jámí, " and my Father, who with his Friends
went forth to salute him, had me carried on the Shoulders
of one of the Family and set down before the Litter of the
Sheikh, who gave a Nosegay into my hand. Sixty Years
have passed, and methinks I now see before me the bright
Image of the Holy Man, and feel the Blessing of his
Aspect, from which I date my after Devotion to that
Brotherhood in which I hope to be enrolled."

So again, when Maulániá Fakhruddín Loristání had
alighted at his Mother's house—" I was then so little that
he set me upon his Knee, and with his Fingers drawing
the Letters of 'ALÍ ' and 'OMAR ' in the Air, laughed with
delight to hear me spell them. He also by his Goodness
sowed in my Heart the Seed of his Devotion, which has
grown to Increase within me—in which I hope to live, and
in which to die. Oh God! Dervish let me live, and Dervish die; and in the Company of the Dervish do Thou
quicken me to life again! "

(41) Jámí first went to a School at Herát; and after|ward
to one founded by the Great Tímúr at Samarcand. There
he not only outstript his Fellow-students in the very En-
cyclopædic Studies of Persian Education, but even puzzled his Doctors in Logic, Astronomy, and Theology;
who, however, with unresenting Gravity welcomed him—
" Lo! a new Light added to our Galaxy! "—And among
them in the wider Field of Samarcand he might have
liked to remain, had not a Dream recalled him to Herát.
A Vision of the Great Súfí Master there, Mohammed
Saaduddín Káshghari, appeared to him in his Sleep, and

bade him return to One who would satisfy all Desire.
Jámí returned to Herát; he saw the Sheikh discoursing
with his Disciples by the Door of the Great Mosque; day
after day passed him by without daring to present himself; but the Master's Eye was upon him; day by day
drew him nearer and nearer—till at last the Sheikh an-
nounces to those about him—" Lo! this Day have I taken
a Falcon in my Snare!"

Under him Jámí began his Súfí Noviciate, with such
Devotion, both to Study and Master, that going, he tells
us, but for one Summer Holiday into the Country, a
single Line sufficed to " lure the Tassel-gentle back
again;"

"Lo! here am I, and Thou look'st on the Rose!"

By-and-by he withdrew, by due course of Súfí Instruc- (42)
tion, into Solitude so long and profound, that on his return to Men he had almost lost the Power of Converse
with them. At last, when duly taught, and duly author-
ised to teach as Súfí Doctor, he yet would not take upon
himself so to do, though solicited by those who had seen
such a Vision of him as had drawn himself to Herát; and
not till the Evening of his Life was he to be seen taking
that place by the Mosque which his departed Master had
been used to occupy before.

Meanwhile he had become Poet, which no doubt winged
his Reputation and Doctrine far and wide through a
People so susceptible of poetic impulse.

" A Thousand times," he says, " I have repented of

[47]

such Employment; but I could no more shirk it than one
can shirk what the Pen of Fate has written on his Forehead "—" As Poet I have resounded through the World;
Heaven filled itself with my Song, and the Bride of Time
adorned her Ears and Neck with the Pearls of my Verse,
whose coming Caravan the Persian Háfiz and Saadí came
forth gladly to salute, and the Indian Khosrau and
Hasan hailed as a Wonder of the World." " The Kings
of India and Rúm greet me by Letter; the Lords of Irák
(43) and Tabríz load me with Gifts; and what|shall I say of
those of Khorásán, who drown me in an Ocean of Muni-
ficence? "

This, though Oriental, is scarcely bombast. Jámí was
honoured by Princes at home and abroad, at the very time
they were cutting one another's Throats; by his own Sultan Abú Saïd; by Hasan Beg of Mesopotamia—" Lord
of Tabríz"—by whom Abú Saïd was defeated, dethroned,
and slain; by Mohammed II. of Turkey—" King of
Rúm "—who in his turn defeated Hasan; and lastly by
Husein Mírzá Baikará, who somehow made away with
the Prince whom Hasan had set up in Abú Saïd's Place
at Herát. Such is the house that Jack builds in Persia.

As Hasan Beg, however—the USUNCASSAN of old
European Annals—is singularly connected with the present Poem, and with probably the most important event in
Jámí's Life, I will briefly follow the Steps that led to
that as well as other Princely Intercourse.

In A. H. 877, A. D. 1472, Jámí set off on his Pilgrimage
to Mecca, as every True Believer who could afford it was

expected once in his Life to do. He, and, on his Account, the Caravan he went with, were honourably and safely escorted through the interjacent Countries by order of their several|Potentates as far as Baghdád. There Jámí *(44)* fell into trouble by the Treachery of a Follower whom he had reproved, and who misquoted his Verse into disparagement of ALÍ, the Darling Imám of Persia. This, getting wind at Baghdád, was there brought to solemn Tribunal. Jámí came victoriously off, his Accuser was pilloried with a dockt Beard in Baghdád Market-place: but the Poet was so ill-pleased with the stupidity of those who had believed the Report, that, in an after Poem, he called for a Cup of Wine to seal up Lips of whose Utterance the Men of Baghdád were unworthy.

After four months' stay there, during which he visited at Helleh the Tomb of Alí's Son Husein, who had fallen at Kerbela, he set forth again—to Najaf, (where he says his Camel sprang forward at sight of Alí's own Tomb)—crossed the Desert in twenty-two days, continually meditating on the Prophet's Glory, to Medina; and so at last to MECCA, where, as he sang in a Ghazal, he went through all Mohammedan Ceremony with a Mystical Understanding of his Own.

He then turned Homeward; was entertained for forty-five days at Damascus, which he left the very Day before the Turkish Mohammed's Envoys came with 5000 Ducats to carry him to Constantinople. On|arriving at Amida, *(45)* the Capital of Mesopotamia, he found War broken out and in full Flame between that Sultan and Hasan Beg,

NOTICE OF JÁMÍ'S LIFE.

King of the Country, who caused Jámí to be honourably escorted through the dangerous Roads to Tabríz; there received him in full Díván, and would fain have him abide at his Court awhile. Jámí, however, was intent on Home, and once more seeing his aged Mother—for *he* was turned of Sixty—and at last reached Herát in the Month of Shaabán, 1473, after the Average Year's Absence.

This is the HASAN, " in Name and Nature *Handsome* " (and so described by some Venetian Ambassadors of the Time), who was Father of YAKÚB BEG, to whom Jámí dedicated the following Poem; and who, after the due murder of an Elder Brother, succeeded to the Throne; till all the Dynasties of "Black and White Sheep " together were swept away a few years after by Ismaïl, Founder of the Sofí Dynasty in Persia.

Arrived at home, Jámí found Husein Mírzá Baikará, last of the Timuridæ, seated on the Throne there, and ready to receive him with open Arms. Nizámuddín Alí Shír, Husein's Vizír, a Poet too, had hailed in Verse the Poet's Advent from Damascus as " The Moon rising in *(46)* the West; " and|they both continued affectionately to honour him as long as he lived.

Jámí sickened of his mortal Illness on the 13th of Moharrem, 1492—a Sunday. His Pulse began to fail on the following Friday, about the Hour of Morning Prayer, and stopped at the very moment when the Muezzin began to call to Evening. He had lived Eighty-one Years. Sultan Husein undertook the pompous Burial of one whose Glory it was to have lived and died in Der-

vish Poverty; the Dignitaries of the Kingdom followed
him to the Grave; where twenty days afterward was recited in presence of the Sultan and his Court an Eulogy
composed by the Vizír, who also laid the first Stone of
a Monument to his Friend's Memory—the first Stone of
" Tarbet'i Jámí," in the Street of Meshhed, a principal
Thoro'fare of the City of Herát. For, says Rosenzweig,
it must be kept in mind that Jámí was reverenced not only
as a Poet and Philosopher, but as a Saint also; who not
only might work a Miracle himself, but leave such a
Power lingering about his Tomb. It was known that an
Arab, who had falsely accused him of selling a Camel he
knew to be unsound, died very shortly after, as Jámí had
predicted, and on the very selfsame spot where the Camel
fell. And that libellous Rogue at Baghdád|—he, put- (47)
ting his hand into his Horse's Ncse-bag to see if the beast
had finisht his Corn, had his Forefinger bitten off by the
same—from which " Verstümmlung " he soon died—I
suppose, as he ought, of Lock-jaw.

The Persians, who are adepts at much elegant Inge-
nuity, are fond of commemorating Events by some anal-
ogous Word or Sentence whose Letters, cabalistically
corresponding to certain Numbers, compose the Date re-
quired. In Jámí's case they have hit upon the word
" Kás," A Cup, whose signification brings his own name
to Memory, and whose relative letters make up his 81
years. They have *Táríkhs* also for remembering the Year
of his Death: Rosenzweig gives some; but Ouseley the
prettiest of all:—

NOTICE OF JÁMÍ'S LIFE.

Dúd az Khorásán bar ámed—
"The smoke" of Sighs "went up from Khorásán."

No Biographer, says Rosenzweig cautiously, records of Jámí's having more than one Wife (Granddaughter of his Master Sheikh) and Four Sons; which, however, are Five too many for the Doctrine of this Poem. Of the Sons, Three died Infant; and the Fourth (born to him in very old Age), and for whom he wrote some Elementary Tracts, and the more famous " Beháristán," lived *(48)* but a few years, and was|remembered by his Father in the Preface to his Khiradnáma-i Iskander—Alexander's Wisdom-book—which perhaps had also been begun for the Boy's Instruction. He had likewise a nephew, one Mauláná Abdullah, who was ambitious of following his Uncle's Footsteps in Poetry. Jámí first dissuaded him; then, by way of trial whether he had a Talent as well as a Taste, bade him imitate Firdausí's Satire on Sháh Mahmúd. The Nephew did so well, that Jámí then encouraged him to proceed; himself wrote the first Couplet of his First (and most celebrated) Poem—Laila and Majnún—

This Book of which the Pen has now laid the Foundation,
May the diploma of Acceptance one day befall it,—

and Abdullah went on to write that and four other Poems which Persia continues to delight in to the present day, remembering their Author under his Takhallus of HÁTIFÍ—" The Voice from Heaven "—and Last of the classic Poets of Persia.

Of Jámí's literary Offspring, Rosenzweig numbers
forty-four. But Shír Khán Lúdí in his " Memoirs of the
Poets," says Ouseley, accounts him Author of *Ninety-
nine* Volumes of Grammar, Poetry, and Theology, which,
he says, " continue to be universally admired in all parts
of the Eastern World, Irán, Túrán, and Hindústán "—
copied some of them into|precious Manuscripts, illumi-   *(49)*
nated with Gold and Painting, by the greatest Penmen
and Artists of the time; one such—the " Beháristán"—
said to have cost some thousands of pounds—autographed
as their own by two Sovereign Descendants of TIMÚR;
and now reposited away from " the Drums and Tramp-
lings " of Oriental Conquest in the tranquil seclusion of
an English library.

With us, his Name is almost wholly associated with
his " Yúsuf and Zulaikhá ; " the " Beháristán " aforesaid :
and this present " Salámán and Absál," which he tells us
is like to be the last product of his Old Age. And these
three Poems count for three of the brother Stars of that
Constellation into which his seven best Mystical Poems
are clustered under the name of " HEFT AURANG "—
those " SEVEN THRONES " to which we of the West and
North give our characteristic name of " Great Bear "
and " Charles's Wain."

This particular Salámán Star, which thus conspicu-
ously figures in Eastern eyes, but is reduced to one of
very inferior magnitude as seen through this English

[53]

Version,—is one of many Allegories under which the
(50) Persian Mystic symbolized an esoteric|doctrine which he
dared not—and probably could not—more intelligibly
reveal. As usual with such Poems in the story-loving
East, the main Fable is intersected at every turn with
some other subsidiary story, more or less illustrative of the
matter in hand: many of these of a comic and grotesque
Character mimicking the more serious, as may the Gra-
cioso of the Spanish Drama. As for the metre of the
Poem, it is the same as that adopted by Attár, Jelálud-
dín and other such Poets—and styled, as I have heard, the
" Metre Royal "—although not having been used by
Firdausí for his Sháh-námeh. Thus it runs:

$$- \cup - - \mid - \cup - - \mid - \cup - \mid$$

a pace which, to those not used to it, seems to bring one
up with too sudden a halt at the end of every line to
promise easy travelling through an Epic. It may be
represented in Monkish Latin Quantity:

> Dum Salámán verba Regis cogitat,
> Pectus illi de profundis æstuat;

or by English accent in two lines that may also plead for
us and our Allegory:

> Of Salámán and of Absál hear the Song;
> Little wants man here below, nor little long.

SALÁMÁN AND ABSÁL.

PRELIMINARY INVOCATION.

Oh Thou, whose Spirit through this universe,
In which Thou dost involve thyself diffused,
Shall so perchance irradiate human clay
That men, suddenly dazzled, lose themselves
In ecstasy before a mortal shrine
Whose Light is but a Shade of the Divine;
Not till thy Secret Beauty through the cheek
Of LAILA smite doth she inflame MAJNÚN;[1]
And not till Thou have kindled SHÍRÍN's Eyes
The hearts of those two Rivals swell with blood.
For Lov'd and Lover are not but by Thee,
Nor Beauty;—mortal Beauty but the veil
Thy Heavenly hides behind, and from itself
Feeds, and our hearts yearn after as a Bride
That glances past us veil'd—but ever so   (52)
That none the veil from what it hides may know.
How long wilt thou continue thus the World
To cozen[2] with the fantom of a veil

[1] *Well-known Types of Eastern Lovers.* SHÍRÍN *and her Suitors fig-*
ure in Sect. xx.
[2] *The Persian Mystics also represent the Deity dicing with Human*
Destiny behind the Curtain.

[55]

From which thou only peepest? I would be
Thy Lover, and thine only—I, mine eyes
Seal'd in the light of Thee to all but Thee,
Yea, in the revelation of Thyself
Lost to Myself, and all that Self is not
Within the Double world that is but One.
Thou lurkest under all the forms of Thought,
Under the form of all Created things;
Look where I may, still nothing I discern
But Thee throughout this Universe, wherein
Thyself Thou dost reflect, and through those eyes
Of him whom MAN thou madest, scrutinize.
To thy Harím DIVIDUALITY
No entrance finds—no word of THIS and THAT;
Do Thou my separate and derivéd Self
Make one with thy Essential! Leave me room
On that Diván which leaves no room for Twain;
Lest, like the simple Arab in the tale,
I grow perplext, oh God! 'twixt "ME" and "THEE;"
(53) If *I*—this Spirit that inspires me whence?
If *THOU*—then what this sensual Impotence?

From the solitary Desert
Up to Baghdád came a simple

Arab; there amid the rout
Grew bewilder'd of the countless
People, hither, thither, running,
Coming, going, meeting, parting,
Clamour, clatter, and confusion,
All about him and about.
Travel-wearied, hubbub-dizzy,
Would the simple Arab fain
Get to sleep—"But then, on waking,
"How," quoth he, "amid so many
"Waking know Myself again?"
So, to make the matter certain,
Strung a gourd about his ankle,
And, into a corner creeping,
Baghdád and Himself and People
Soon were blotted from his brain.
But one that heard him and divined
His purpose, slily crept behind;
From the Sleeper's ankle clipping,*
Round his own the pumpkin tied,   (54)
And laid him down to sleep beside.
By and by the Arab waking
Looks directly for his Signal—
Sees it on another's Ankle—
Cries aloud, "Oh Good-for-nothing

*"Slipping." (Third edition.)

[57   ]

"Rascal to perplex me so!
"That by you I am bewilder'd,
"Whether I be I or no!
"If I—the Pumpkin why on You?
"If You—*then Where am I, and* Who?"

AND yet, how long, O Jámí, stringing Verse,
Pearl after pearl, on that old Harp of thine?
Year after year attuning some new Song,
The breath of some old Story?[1]   Life is gone,
And that last song is not the last; my Soul
Is spent—and still a Story to be told!
And I, whose back is crooked as the Harp
I still keep tuning through the Night till Day!
That Harp untuned by Time—the harper's hand
Shaking with Age—how shall the harper's hand
Repair its cunning, and the sweet old harp
(55) Be modulated as of old?   Methinks
'Twere time to break and cast it in the fire;
The vain old harp, that, breathing from its strings
No music more to charm the ears of men,
May, from its scented ashes, as it burns,
Breathe resignation to the Harper's soul,
Now that his body looks to dissolution.

[1] *"Yúsuf and Zulaikhá," "Laila and Majnún," &c.*

[58]

My teeth fall out—my two eyes see no more
Till by Feringhí glasses turn'd to four; [1]
Pain sits with me sitting behind my knees,
From which I hardly rise unhelpt of hand;
I bow down to my root, and like a Child
Yearn, as is likely, to my Mother Earth,
Upon whose bosom I shall cease to weep,
And on my Mother's bosom fall asleep. [2]

The House in ruin, and its music heard
No more within, nor at the door of speech,
Better in silence and oblivion
To fold me head and foot, remembering
What THE VOICE whisper'd in the Master's [3] ear—
" No longer think of Rhyme, but think of ME! "—   (56)
Of WHOM?—Of HIM whose Palace the SOUL is,
And Treasure-house—who notices and knows
Its income and out-going, and *then* comes
To fill it when the Stranger is departed.
Yea; but whose Shadow being Earthly Kings,
Their Attributes, their Wrath and Favour, His,—
Lo! in the meditation of His glory,

[1] *First notice of Spectacles in Oriental Poetry, perhaps.*
[2] *The same Figure is found in Chaucer's "Pardoner's Tale," and, I think, in other Western poems of that era.*
[3] *Mohammed Saaduddín Káshgharí, spoken of in Notice of Jámí's life, p. 46.*
["Jeláluddín—Author of the "Mesnavi." (Third edition.)]

[59   ]

SALÁMAN AND ABSÁL.

The SHÁH [1] whose subject upon Earth I am,

As he of Heaven's, comes on me unaware,

And suddenly arrests me for his due.

Therefore for one last travel, and as brief

As may become the feeble breath of Age,

My weary pen once more drinks of the well,

Whence, of the Mortal writing, I may read

Anticipation of the Invisible.

One who travell'd in the Desert

Saw MAJNÚN where he was sitting

All alone like a Magician

   Tracing Letters in the Sand,

"Oh distracted Lover! writing

(57)   *"What the Sword-wind of the Desert*

"Undeciphers so that no one

   "After you shall understand."

MAJNÚN answer'd—"I am writing

"Only for myself, and only

" ' LAILA,'—If for ever ' LAILA '

"Writing, in that Word a Volume,

"Over which for ever poring,

"From her very Name I sip

"In Fancy, till I drink, her Lip."

[1] YAKÚB BEG: *to whose protection Jámí owed a Song of gratitude.*

[60]

THE STORY.

PART I.

A SHÁH there was who ruled the realm of Yún,[1]
And wore the Ring of Empire of Sikander;
And in his reign A SAGE, of such report
For Insight reaching quite beyond the Veil,
That Wise men from all quarters of the World,
To catch the jewel falling from his lips
Out of the secret treasure as he went,
Went in a girdle round him.—Which the SHÁH
Observing, took him to his secresy;
Stirr'd not a step, nor set design afoot,
Without the Prophet's sanction; till, so counsell'd,
From Káf to Káf[2] reach'd his Dominion:
No People, and no Prince that over them
The ring of Empire wore, but under his
Bow'd down in Battle; rising then in Peace
Under his Justice grew, secure from wrong,
And in their strength was his Dominion strong.

[1] Or "YAVAN," Son of Japhet, from whom the Country was called "YÚNAN,"—IONIA, meant by the Persians to express GREECE generally. Sikander is, of course, Alexander the Great.
[2] The Fabulous Mountain supposed by Asiatics to surround the World, binding the Horizon on all sides.

(59) The SHÁH that has not Wisdom in himself,
Nor has a Wise one for his Counsellor,
The wand of his Authority falls short,
And his Dominion crumbles at the base.
For he, discerning not the characters
Of Tyranny and Justice, confounds both,
Making the World a desert, and Redress
A fantom-water of the Wilderness.

———————

God said to the Prophet David—
"David, whom I have exalted
"From the sheep to be my People's
"Shepherd, by your Justice my
"Revelation justify.
"Lest the misbelieving—yea,
"The Fire-adoring, Princes rather
"Be my Prophets, who fulfil,
"Knowing not my WORD, my WILL."

———————

ONE night THE SHÁH of Yúnan as he sate
Contemplating his measureless extent
Of Empire, and the glory wherewithal,
(60) As with a garment robed, he ruled alone;
Then found he nothing wanted to his heart
Unless a Son, who, while he lived, might share,

And, after him, his robe of Empire wear.

And then he turned him to THE SAGE, and said:

" O Darling of the soul of IFLATÚN; [1]

" To whom with all his school ARISTO bows;

" Yea, thou that an ELEVENTH to the TEN

" INTELLIGENCES addest: Thou hast read

" The yet unutter'd secret of my Heart,

" Answer—Of all that man desires of God

" Is any blessing greater than a Son?

" Man's prime Desire; by whom his name and he

" Shall live beyond himself; by whom his eyes

" Shine living, and his dust with roses blows.

" A Foot for thee to stand on, and an Arm

" To lean by; sharp in battle as a sword;

" Salt of the banquet-table; and a tower

" Of salutary counsel in Diván;

" One in whose youth a Father shall prolong

" His years, and in his strength continue strong."

When the shrewd SAGE had heard THE SHÁH's discourse

In commendation of a Son, he said: (61)

" Thus much of a *Good* Son, whose wholesome growth

" Approves the root he grew from.   But for one

" Kneaded of *Evil*—well, could one revoke

" His generation, and as early pull

[1] *Iflatún, Plato; Aristo, Aristotle: both renowned in the East to this Day.   For the Ten Intelligences, see Appendix.*

" Him and his vices from the string of Time.

" Like Noah's, puff'd with insolence and pride,

" Who, reckless of his Father's warning call,

" Was by the voice of ALLAH from the door

" Of refuge in his Father's Ark debarr'd,

" And perish'd in the Deluge.[1]   And as none

 " Who long for children may their children choose,

" Beware of teazing Allah for a Son,

 " Whom having, you may have to pray to lose."

 Sick at heart for want of Children,
 Ran before the Saint a Fellow,
 Catching at his garment, crying,
  "Master, hear and help me! Pray
  "That ALLAH *from the barren clay*
 "Raise me up a fresh young Cypress,
 "Who my longing eyes may lighten,
 "And not let me like a vapour
(62) *"Unremember'd pass away."*
 But the Dervish said—"Consider;
  "Wisely let the matter rest
 "In the hands of ALLAH *wholly,*
 "Who, whatever we are after,
  "Understands our business best."

[1] *See Note in Appendix I.*

[64]

FOURTH
EDITION

Still the man persisted—"Master,

"I shall perish in my longing:

"Help, and set my prayer a-going!"

   Then the Dervish raised his hand—

   From the mystic Hunting-land

Of Darkness to the Father's arms

   A musky Fawn of China drew—

A Boy—who, when the shoot of Passion

   In his Nature planted grew,

Took to drinking, dicing, drabbing.

From a corner of the house-top

Ill-insulting honest women,

Dagger-drawing on the husband;

   And for many a city-brawl

Still before the Cadi summon'd,

   Still the Father pays for all.

Day and night the youngster's doings

Such—the city's talk and scandal;

Neither counsel, threat, entreaty,

Moved him—till the desperate Father

Once more to the Dervish running, (63)

Catches at his garment—crying—

"Oh my only Hope and Helper!

"One more Prayer! That God, who laid,

"Would take this trouble from my head!"

[65]

But the Saint replied—"Remember
"How that very Day I warn'd you
"Not with blind petition ALLAH
"Trouble to your own confusion;
"Unto whom remains no more
"To pray for, save that He may pardon
"What so rashly pray'd before."

———

" So much for the result; and for the means—
" Oh SHÁH, who would not be himself a slave,
" Which SHÁH least should, and of an appetite
" Among the basest of his slaves enslaved—
" Better let Azrael find him on his throne
" Of Empire sitting childless and alone,
" Than his untainted Majesty resign
" To that seditious drink, of which one draught
" Still for another and another craves,
" Till it become a noose to draw the Crown
(*64*) " From off thy brows—about thy lips a ring,
" Of which the rope is in a Woman's hand,
" To lead thyself the road of Nothing down.
" For what is *She?* A foolish, faithless thing—
" A very Káfir in rapacity;
" Robe her in all the rainbow-tinted woof
" Of Susa, shot with rays of sunny Gold;

[66]

" Deck her with jewel thick as Night with star;

" Pamper her appetite with Houri fruit

" Of Paradise, and fill her jewell'd cup

" From the green-mantled Prophet's Well of Life—

" One little twist of temper—all your cost

" Goes all for nothing: and, as for yourself—

" Look! On your bosom she may lie for years;

" But, get you gone a moment out of sight,

" And she forgets you—worse, if, as you turn,

" Her eyes on any younger Lover light."

Once upon the Throne together

Telling one another Secrets,

Sate SULAYMÁN *and* BALKÍS; [1]

The Hearts of both were turn'd to Truth, (65)

Unsullied by Deception.

First the King of Faith SULAYMÁN

   Spoke—"However just and wise

" Reported, none of all the many

"Suitors to my palace thronging

   "But afar I scrutinize;

"And He who comes not empty-handed

   "Grows to Honour in mine Eyes."

After this, BALKIS *a Secret*

----

[1] *Solomon and the Queen of Sheba, who, it appears, is no worse in one way than Solomon in another, unless in Oriental Eyes.*

SALÁMÁN AND ABSÁL.

From her hidden bosom utter'd,
Saying—"Never night or morning
"Comely Youth before me passes
"Whom I look not after, longing"—

" If this, as wise Firdausí says, the curse
" Of better women, what then of the worse? "

THE SAGE his satire ended; and THE SHÁH,
Determined on his purpose, but the means
Resigning to Supreme Intelligence,
With Magic-mighty Wisdom his own WILL
Colleagued, and wrought his own accomplishment.
For Lo! from Darkness came to Light A CHILD,
Of carnal composition unattaint;
(66) A Perfume from the realm of Wisdom wafted;
A Rosebud blowing on the Royal stem;
The crowning Jewel of the Crown; a Star
Under whose augury triumph'd the Throne.
For whom dividing, and again in one
Whole perfect Jewel re-uniting, those
Twin Jewel-words SALÁMAT and ASMÁN,[1]
They hail'd him by the title of SALÁMÁN.
And whereas from no Mother milk he drew,
They chose for him a Nurse—her name ABSÁL—

---

[1] SALÁMAT, *Security from Evil;* ASMÁN, *Heaven.*

So young, the opening roses of her breast
But just had budded to an infant's lip;
So beautiful, as from the silver line
Dividing the musk-harvest of her hair
Down to her foot that trampled crowns of Kings,
A Moon of beauty full; who thus elect
Should in the garment of her bounty fold
SALÁMÁN of auspicious augury,
Should feed him with the flowing of her breast.
And, once her eyes had open'd upon Him,
They closed to all the world beside, and fed
For ever doating on her Royal jewel
Close in his golden cradle casketed:
Opening and closing which her day's delight,
To gaze upon his heart-inflaming cheek,—   (67)
Upon the Babe whom, if she could, she would
Have cradled as the Baby of her eye.[1]
In rose and musk she wash'd him—to his lip
Press'd the pure sugar from the honeycomb;
And when, day over, she withdrew her milk,
She made, and having laid him in, his bed,
Burn'd all night like a taper o'er his head.

And still as Morning came, and as he grew,
Finer than any bridal-puppet, which

[1] *Literally,* Mardumak—*the* Mannikin, *or* Pupil, *of the* Eye, *corresponding to the Image so frequently used by our old Poets.*

[69]

SALÁMÁN AND ABSÁL.

To prove another's love a woman sends,[1]
She trick'd him up—with fresh Collyrium dew
Touch'd his narcissus eyes—the musky locks
Divided from his forehead—and embraced
With gold and ruby girdle his fine waist.

So for seven years she rear'd and tended him:
Nay, when his still-increasing moon of Youth
Into the further Sign of Manhood pass'd
Pursued him yet, till full fourteen his years,
Fourteen-day full the beauty of his face,
(68) That rode high in a hundred thousand hearts.
For, when SALÁMÁN was but half-lance high,
Lance-like he struck a wound in every one,
And shook down splendour round him like a Sun.

Soon as the Lord of Heav'n had sprung his horse
Over horizon into the blue field,
SALÁMÁN kindled with the wine of sleep,
Mounted a barb of fire for the Maidán;
He and a troop of Princes—Kings in blood,
Kings in the kingdom-troubling tribe of beauty,
All young in years and courage,[2] bat in hand
Gallop'd a-field, toss'd down the golden ball

[1] See Appendix.
[2] The same Persian Word signifying Youth and Courage.

[70]

And chased, so many crescent Moons a full;[1]
And, all alike intent upon the Game,
SALÁMÁN still would carry from them all
The prize, and shouting " Hál! " drive home the ball.

This done, SALÁMÁN bent him as a bow
To Archery—from Masters of the craft
Call'd for an unstrung bow—himself the cord   (69)
Fitted unhelpt,[2] and nimbly with his hand
Twanging made cry, and drew it to his ear;
Then, fixing the three-feather'd fowl, discharged:
And whether aiming at the fawn a-foot,
Or bird on wing, direct his arrow flew,
Like the true Soul that cannot but go true.

WHEN night came, that releases man from toil,
He play'd the chess of social intercourse;
Prepared his banquet-hall like Paradise,
Summon'd his Houri-faced musicians,
And, when his brain grew warm with wine, the veil
Flung off him of reserve; taking a harp,

---

[1] *See Appendix.*
[2] *Bows being so gradually stiffened, according to the age and strength
of the Archer, as at last to need five Hundred-weight of pressure to
bend, says an old Translation of Chardin, who describes all the pro-
cess up to bringing up the string to the ear, "as if to hang it there"
before shooting. Then the first trial was, who could shoot highest:
then, the mark, &c.*

[71]

SALÁMÁN AND ABSÁL.

Between its dry string and his finger quick
Struck fire: or catching up a lute, as if
A child for chastisement, would pinch its ear
To wailing that should agéd eyes make weep.
(70) Now like the Nightingale he sang alone;
Now with another lip to lip; and now
Together blending voice and instrument;
And thus with his associates night he spent.

His Soul rejoiced in knowledge of all kind;
The fine edge of his Wit would split a hair,
And in the noose of apprehension catch
A meaning ere articulate in word;
Close as the knitted jewel of Parwín
His jewel Verse he strung; his Rhetoric
Enlarging like the Mourners of the Bier.[1]
And when he took the nimble reed in hand
To run the errand of his Thought along
Its paper field—the character he traced,
Fine on the lip of Youth as the first hair,
Drove Penmen, as that Lovers, to despair.

His Bounty like a Sea was fathomless
That bubbled up with jewel, and flung pearl

---

[1] *The Pleiades and the Great Bear. This is otherwise prettily applied
in the Anvári Soheili—"When one grows poor, his Friends, heretofore
compact as* THE PLEIADES, *disperse wide asunder as* THE MOURNERS."

Where'er it touch'd, but drew not back again;
It was a Heav'n that rain'd on all below *(71)*
Dirhems for drops—

  BUT here that inward Voice
Arrested and rebuked me—" Foolish Jámí!
" Wearing that indefatigable pen
" In celebration of an alien SHÁH
" Whose Throne, not grounded in the Eternal World,
" If YESTERDAY it were, TO-DAY is not,
" TO-MORROW cannot be." [1] But I replied;
" O Fount of Light!—under an alien name
" I shadow One upon whose head the Crown
" WAS and yet Is, and SHALL BE; whose Firmán
" The Kingdoms Sev'n of this World, and the Seas,
" And the Sev'n Heavens, alike are subject to.
" Good luck to him who under other Name
" Instructed us that Glory to disguise
" To which the Initiate scarce dare lift his eyes."

 Sate a Lover in a Garden
 All alone, apostrophizing

[1] *The Hero of the Story being of* YÚNAN—IONIA, *or* GREECE *generally (the Persian Geography not being very precise)—and so not of* THE FAITH.

[73]

(72)   *Many a flower and shrub about him,*
         And the lights of Heav'n above.
Nightingaling thus, a Noodle
Heard him, and, completely puzzled,
"What," quoth he, "and you a Lover,
"Raving, not about your Mistress,
"But about the stars and roses—
     "What have these to do with Love?"
Answer'd he: "Oh thou that aimest
"Wide of Love, and Lovers' language
   "Wholly misinterpreting;
"Sun and Moon are but my Lady's
   "Self, as any Lover knows;
"Hyacinth I said, and meant her
   "Hair—her cheek was in the rose—
"And I myself the wretched weed
   "That in her cypress shadow grows."

AND now the cypress stature of Salámán
Had reached his top, and now to blossom full
The garden of his Beauty; and Absál,
Fairest of hers, as of his fellows he
The fairest, long'd to gather from the tree.
(73) But, for that flower upon the lofty stem
Of Glory grew to which her hand fell short,

[74]

She now with woman's sorcery began
To conjure as she might within her reach.
The darkness of her eyes she darken'd round
With surma, to benight him in mid day,
And over them adorn'd and arch'd the bows [1]
To wound him there when lost: her musky locks
Into so many snaky ringlets curl'd,
In which Temptation nestled o'er the cheek
Whose rose she kindled with vermilion dew,
And then one subtle grain of musk laid there,[2]
The bird of that belovéd heart to snare.
Sometimes in passing with a laugh would break
The pearl-enclosing ruby of her lips;
Or, busied in the room, as by mischance
Would let the lifted sleeve disclose awhile
The vein of silver running up within:
Or, rising as in haste, her golden anklets
Clash, at whose sudden summons to bring down
Under her silver feet the golden Crown.
Thus, by innumerable witcheries,
She went about soliciting his eyes,   (74)
Through which she knew the robber unaware
Steals in, and takes the bosom by surprise.

[1] *With dark Indigo-paint, as the Archery Bow with a thin Papyrus-like Bark.*
[2] *A Patch, sc.*—"Noir comme le Musc." *De Sacy.*

[75]

Burning with her love ZULAIKHÁ
Built a chamber, wall and ceiling
Blank as an untarnisht mirror,
Spotless as the heart of YÚSUF.
Then she made a cunning painter
Multiply her image round it;
Not an inch of wall or ceiling
But re-echoing her beauty.
Then amid them all in all her
Glory sate she down, and sent for
    YÚSUF—*she began a tale*
    Of Love—and lifted up her veil.
Bashfully beneath her burning
Eyes he turn'd away; but turning
Wheresoever, still about him
Saw ZULAIKHÁ, *still* ZULAIKHÁ,
Still, without a veil, ZULAIKHÁ.

(75)   *But a Voice as if from Canaan*
Call'd him; and a Hand from Darkness
    Touch'd; and ere a living Lip
Through the mirage of bewilder'd
Eyes seduced him, he recoiled,
    And let the skirt of danger slip.

PART II.

ALAS for those who having tasted once
Of that forbidden vintage of the lips
That, press'd and pressing, from each other draw
The draught that so intoxicates them both,
That, while upon the wings of Day and Night
Time rustles on, and Moons do wax and wane,
As from the very Well of Life they drink,
And, drinking, fancy they shall never drain.
But rolling Heaven from his ambush whispers,
"So in my license is it not set down:
"Ah for the sweet societies I make
"At Morning, and before the Nightfall break;
"Ah for the bliss that coming Night fills up,
"And Morn looks in to find an empty Cup!"

Once in Baghdád a poor Arab,
After weary days of fasting,
Into the Khalífah's banquet-
Chamber, where, aloft in State
HARÚN the Great at supper sate,
*   Push'd and pushing, with the throng,*
Got before a perfume-breathing

[77]

SALÁMÁN AND ABSÁL.

Pasty, like the lip of SHÍRÍN
Luscious, or the Poet's song.
Soon as seen, the famisht clown
Seizes up and swallows down.
Then his mouth undaunted wiping—
"Oh Khalífah, hear me swear,
"While I breathe the dust of Baghdád,
"Ne'er at any other Table
"Than at Thine to sup or dine."
Grimly laugh'd HARÚN, *and answer'd:*
  "Fool! who think'st to arbitrate
  "What is in the hands of Fate—
  "Take, and thrust him from the Gate!"

WHILE a full Year was counted by the Moon,
SALÁMÁN and ABSÁL rejoiced together,
And neither SHÁH nor SAGE his face beheld.
They question'd those about him, and from them
Heard something: then himself to presence summon'd,
And all the truth was told. Then SAGE and SHÁH
Struck out with hand and foot in his redress.
(78) And first with REASON, which is also best;
REASON that rights the wanderer; that completes
The imperfect; REASON that resolves the knot
Of either world, and sees beyond the Veil.
[78]

For REASON is the fountain from of old
From which the Prophets drew, and none beside:
Who boasts of other inspiration, lies—
There are no other Prophets than THE WISE.

AND first THE SHÁH:— " SALÁMÁN, Oh my Soul,
" Light of the eyes of my Prosperity,
" And making bloom the court of Hope with rose;
" Year after year, SALÁMÁN, like a bud
" That cannot blow, my own blood I devour'd,
" Till, by the seasonable breath of God,
" At last I blossom'd into thee, my Son;
" Oh, do not wound me with a dagger thron;
" Let not the full-blown rose of Royalty
" Be left to wither in a hand unclean.
" For what thy proper pastime? Bat in hand
" To mount and manage RAKHSH ¹ along the Field;
" Not, with no weapon but a wanton curl   (79)
" Idly reposing on a silver breast.
" Go, fly thine arrow at the antelope
" And lion—let me not My lion see
" Slain by the arrow eyes of a ghazál.
" Go, challenge ZÁL or RUSTAM to the Field,

¹ "LIGHTNING." The name of RUSTAM's famous Horse in the SHÁH-NÁMEH.

" And smite the warriors' neck; not, flying them,

" Beneath a woman's foot submit thine own.

" O wipe the woman's henna from thy hand,

" Withdraw thee from the minion [1] who from thee

" Dominion draws, and draws me with thee down;

" Years have I held my head aloft, and all

" For Thee—Oh shame if thou prepare my Fall! "

When before SHIRÚYEH's *dagger*

    KAI KHUSRAU,[2] *his Father, fell,*

    He declared this Parable—

(80)   *"Wretch!—There was a branch that waxing*

    "Wanton o'er the root he drank from,

    "At a draught the living water

      "Drain'd wherewith himself to crown;

    "Died the root—and with him died

      "The branch—and barren was brought down! "

THE SHÁH ceased counsel, and THE SAGE began.

" O last new vintage of the Vine of Life

[1] "SHÁH," *and* "SHÁHID" *(A Mistress).*

[2] KHUSRAU PARVÍZ *(Chosroe The Victorious), Son of* NOSHÍRVÁN *The Great; slain, after Thirty Years of prosperous Reign, by his Son* SHIRÚYEH, *who, according to some, was in love with his Father's mistress* SHÍRÍN. *See further on one of the most dramatic Tragedies in Persian history.*

" Planted in Paradise; Oh Master-stroke,

" And all-concluding flourish of the Pen

" Kun fa-yakún;[1] Thyself prime Archetype,

" And ultimate Accomplishment of Man!

" The Almighty hand, that out of common earth

" Thy mortal outward to the perfect form

" Of Beauty moulded, in the fleeting dust

" Inscribed Himself, and in thy bosom set

" A mirror to reflect Himself in Thee.

" Let not that dust by rebel passion blown

" Obliterate that character: nor let

" That Mirror, sullied by the breath impure, *(81)*

" Or form of carnal beauty fore-possest,

" Be made incapable of the Divine.

" Supreme is thine Original degree,

" Thy Star upon the top of Heaven; but Lust

" Will bring it down, down even to the Dust!"

Quoth a Muezzín to the crested
Cock—"Oh Prophet of the Morning,
"Never Prophet like to you
"Prophesied of Dawn, nor Muezzín
"With so shrill a voice of warning

[1] "Be! and it is."—*The famous Word of Creation stolen from Genesis by the Kurán.*

[81]

"Woke the sleeper to confession

"Crying, 'Lá ALLÁH ILLÁ 'LLAH,

*"*MUHAMMAD RASÚLUHU.'* [1]

"One, methinks, so rarely gifted

"Should have prophesied and sung

"In Heav'n, the Bird of Heav'n among,

"Not with these poor hens about him,

"Raking in a heap of dung."

"And," replied the Cock, "in Heaven

"Once I was; but by my foolish

(82)   *"Lust to this uncleanly living*

"With my sorry mates about me

"Thus am fallen.   Otherwise,

"I were prophesying Dawn

"Before the gates of Paradise." [2]

——————

Of all the Lover's sorrows, next to that
Of Love by Love forbidden, is the voice
Of Friendship turning harsh in Love's reproof,
And overmuch of Counsel—whereby Love
Grows stubborn, and recoiling unsupprest
Within, devours the heart within the breast.

[1] *"There is no God but God; Muhammad is his Prophet."*
[2] *Jámí, as, may be, other Saintly Doctors, kept soberly to one Wife.
But wherefore, under the Law of Muhammad, should the Cock be
selected (as I suppose he is) for a "Caution," because of his indul-
gence in Polygamy, however unusual among Birds?*

SALÁMÁN heard; his Soul came to his lips;

Reproaches struck not ABSÁL out of him,

But drove Confusion in; bitter became

The drinking of the sweet draught of Delight,

And wan'd the splendour of his Moon of Beauty.

His breath was Indignation, and his heart

Bled from the arrow, and his anguish grew.   (83)

How bear it?—By the hand of Hatred dealt,

Easy to meet—and deal with, blow for blow;

But from Love's hand which one must not requite,

And cannot yield to—what resource but Flight?

Resolv'd on which, he victuall'd and equipp'd

A Camel, and one night he led it forth,

And mounted—he with ABSÁL at his side,

Like sweet twin almonds in a single shell.

And Love least murmurs at the narrow space

That draws him close and closer in embrace.

———————

When the Moon of Canaan YÚSUF

In the prison of Egypt darken'd,

Nightly from her spacious Palace-

Chamber, and its rich array,

Stole ZULAIKHÁ *like a fantom*

To the dark and narrow dungeon

Where her buried Treasure lay.

[83]

Then to those about her wond'ring—
"Were my Palace," she replied,
"Wider than Horizon-wide,
"It were narrower than an Ant's eye,
"Were my Treasure not inside:
"And an Ant's eye, if but there
"My lover, Heaven's horizon were."

(84)

SIX days SALÁMÁN on the Camel rode,
And then the hissing arrows of reproof
Were fallen far behind; and on the Seventh
He halted on the Seashore; on the shore
Of a great Sea that reaching like a floor
Of rolling Firmament below the Sky's
From KÁF to KÁF, to GAU and MÁHÍ[1] down
Descended, and its Stars were living eyes.
The Face of it was as it were a range
Of moving Mountains; or a countless host
Of Camels trooping tumultuously up,
Host over host, and foaming at the lip.
Within, innumerable glittering things

[1] *Bull and Fish—the lowest Substantial Base of Earth.* "He first
*made the Mountains; then cleared the Face of the Earth from Sea;
then fixed it fast on Gau; Gau on Máhí; and Máhí on Air; and Air on
what? on* NOTHING; *Nothing on Nothing, all is Nothing.—Enough."
Attár; quoted in De Sacy's Pendnamah, xxxv.*

Sharp as cut Jewels, to the sharpest eye

Scarce visible, hither and thither slipping, *(85)*

As silver scissors slice a blue brocade;

But should the Dragon coil'd in the abyss [1]

Emerge to light, his starry counter-sign

Would shrink into the depth of Heav'n aghast.

SALÁMÁN eyed the moving wilderness

On which he thought, once launcht, no foot, nor eye

Should ever follow; forthwith he devised

Of sundry scented woods along the shore

A little shallop like a Quarter-moon,

Wherein Absál and He like Sun and Moon

Enter'd as into some Celestial Sign;

That, figured like a bow, but arrow-like

In flight, was feather'd with a little sail,

And, pitcht upon the water like a duck,

So with her bosom sped to her Desire.

When they had sail'd their vessel for a Moon,

And marr'd their beauty with the wind o' the Sea,

Suddenly in mid sea reveal'd itself *(86)*

---

[1] *The Sidereal Dragon, whose Head, according to the Pauránic (or poetic) astronomers of the East, devoured the Sun and Moon in Eclipse. "But we know," said Rámachandra to Sir W. Jones, "that the supposed Head and Tail of the Dragon mean only the Nodes, or points formed by intersections of the Ecliptic and the Moon's Orbit." Sir W. Jones' Works, vol. iv., p. 74.*

SALÁMÁN AND ABSÁL.

An Isle, beyond imagination fair;
An Isle that all was Garden; not a Flower,
Nor Bird of plumage like the flower, but there;
Some like the Flower, and others like the Leaf;
Some, as the Pheasant and the Dove adorn'd
With crown and collar, over whom, alone,
The jewell'd Peacock like a Sultan shone;
While the Musicians, and among them Chief
The Nightingale, sang hidden in the trees
Which, arm in arm, from fingers quivering
With any breath of air, fruit of all kind
Down scatter'd in profusion to their feet,
Where fountains of sweet water ran between,
And Sun and shadow chequer-chased the green.
Here Iram-garden seem'd in secresy
Blowing the rosebud of its Revelation; [1]
Or Paradise, forgetful of the dawn
Of Audit, lifted from her face the veil.

SALÁMÁN saw the Isle, and thought no more
Of Further—there with ABSÁL he sate down,
ABSÁL and He together side by side
Together like the Lily and the Rose,
(87) Together like the Soul and Body, one.
Under its trees in one another's arms

[1] *Note in Appendix.*

[86]

They slept—they drank its fountains hand in hand—
Paraded with the Peacock—raced the Partridge—
Chased the green Parrot for his stolen fruit,
Or sang divisions with the Nightingale.
There was the Rose without a thorn, and there
The Treasure and no Serpent[1] to beware—
Oh think of such a Mistress at your side
In such a Solitude, and none to chide!

———————

Said to WÁMIK *one who never*
Knew the Lover's passion—" Why
"Solitary thus and silent
"Solitary places haunting,
"Like a Dreamer, like a Spectre,
    "Like a thing about to die? "
WÁMIK *answer'd—"Meditating*
"Flight with Azrá[1] *to the Desert:*
"There by so remote a Fountain
    "That, whichever way one travell'd,
"League on league, one yet should never   (88)
"See the face of Man; for ever
"There to gaze on my Belovéd;
    "Gaze, till Gazing out of Gazing

[1] *The supposed guardian of buried treasure.*
[2] *Wámik and Azrá (Lover and Virgin) two typical Lovers.*

[87]

"Grew to Being Her I gaze on,
*"*She* and* I *no more, but in One*
"Undivided Being blended.
"All that is by Nature twain
"Fears, or suffers by, the pain
"Of Separation: Love is only
   "Perfect when itself transcends
"Itself, and, one with that it loves,
   "In undivided Being blends."

————

WHEN by and by the SHÁH was made aware
Of that heart-breaking Flight, his royal robe
He chang'd for ashes, and his Throne for dust,
And wept awhile in darkness and alone.
Then rose; and, taking counsel from the SAGE,
Pursuit set everywhere afoot: but none
Could trace the footstep of the flying Deer.
Then from his secret Art the Sage-Vizyr
A Magic Mirror made; a Mirror like
The bosom of All-wise Intelligence
(89) Reflecting in its mystic compass all
Within the sev'n-fold volume of the World
Involv'd; and, looking in that Mirror's face,
The SHÁH beheld the face of his Desire.
Beheld those Lovers, like that earliest pair

[88]

Of Lovers, in this other Paradise
So far from human eyes in the mid sea,
And yet within the magic glass so near
As with a finger one might touch them, isled.
THE SHÁH beheld them; and compassion touch'd
His eyes and anger died upon his lips;
And arm'd with Righteous Judgment as he was,
Yet, seeing those two Lovers with one lip
Drinking that cup of Happiness and Tears [1]
In which Farewell had never yet been flung,[2]
He paused for their Repentance to recall
The lifted arm that was to shatter all.

The Lords of Wrath have perish'd by the blow
Themselves had aim'd at others long ago.
Draw not in haste the sword, which Fate, may be,
Will sheathe, hereafter to be drawn on Thee.

FARHÁD, *who the shapeless mountain*   (90)
Into human likeness moulded,
Under SHÍRÍN's *eyes as slavish*
Potters' earth himself became.

[1] Κρατῆρα μακρὸν ἡδονῆς καὶ δακρύων
Κιρνῶντες ἐξέπινον ἄχρις ἐς μέθην.
From Theodorus Prodromas, as quoted by Sir W. Jones.
[2] *A pebble flung into a Cup being a signal for a company to break up.*

[89]

SÁLÁMAN AND ABSÁL.

Then the secret fire of jealous
Frenzy, catching and devouring
KAI KHUSRAU, broke into flame.

With that ancient Hag of Darkness
Plotting, at the midnight Banquet
FARHÁD's golden cup he poison'd,
And in SHÍRÍN's eyes alone
Reign'd—But Fate that Fate revenges,
Arms SHIRÚYEH with the dagger
That at once from SHÍRÍN tore,
And hurl'd him lifeless from his throne.[1]

(91) BUT as the days went on, and still THE SHÁH
Beheld his Son how in the Woman lost,
And still the Crown that should adorn his head,
And still the Throne that waited for his foot,
Both trampled under by a base desire,
Of which the Soul was still unsatisfied—
Then from the sorrow of THE SHÁH fell Fire;
To Gracelessness ungracious he became,

[1] *One story is that Khusrau had promised that if Farhád cut through
a Mountain, and brought a Stream through, Shírín would be his.
Farhád was on the point of achieving his work, when Khusrau sent an
old Woman (here, perhaps, purposely confounded with Fate) to tell
him Shírín was dead; whereon Farhád threw himself headlong from
the Rock. The Sculpture at Beysitún (or Besitún), where Rawlinson
has deciphered Darius and Xerxes, was traditionally called Farhád's.*

And, quite to shatter that rebellious lust,
Upon SALÁMÁN all his WILL, with all [1]
His SAGE-VIZYR's Might-magic arm'd, discharged.
And Lo! SALÁMÁN to his Mistress turn'd,
But could not reach her—look'd and look'd again,
And palpitated tow'rd her—but in vain!
Oh Misery! As to the Bankrupt's eyes
The Gold he may not finger! or the Well
To him who sees a-thirst, and cannot reach,
Or Heav'n above reveal'd to those in Hell!
Yet when SALÁMÁN's anguish was extreme,
The door of Mercy open'd, and he saw
That Arm he knew to be his Father's reacht
To lift him from the pit in which he lay:
Timidly tow'rd his Father's eyes his own
　He lifted, pardon-pleading, crime-confest, *(92)*
And drew once more to that forsaken Throne,
　As the stray bird one day will find her nest.

———

One was asking of a Teacher,
"How a Father his reputed
　"Son for his should recognise?"
Said the Master, "By the stripling,
　"As he grows to manhood, growing

[1]*He Mesmerises him!—See also further on this Power of the* WILL.

"Like to his reputed Father,
"Good or Evil, Fool or Wise.

"Lo the disregarded Darnel
"With itself adorns the Wheat-field,
"And for all the vernal season
"Satisfies the farmer's eye;
"But the hour of harvest coming,
"And the thrasher by and by,
"Then a barren ear shall answer,
"'Darnel, and no Wheat, am I.'"

---

(93) YET Ah for that poor Lover! "Next the curse
"Of Love by Love forbidden, nothing worse
"Than Friendship turn'd in Love's reproof unkind,
"And Love from Love divorcing"—Thus I said:
Alas, a worse, and worse, is yet behind—
Love's back-blow of Revenge for having fled!

SALÁMÁN bow'd his forehead to the dust
Before his Father; to his Father's hand
Fast—but yet fast, and faster, to his own
Clung one, who by no tempest of reproof
Or wrath might be dissever'd from the stem
She grew to: till, between Remorse and Love,
He came to loathe his Life and long for Death.

[92]

And, as from him *She* would not be divorced,
With Her he fled again: he fled—but now
To no such Island centred in the sea
As lull'd them into Paradise before;
But to the Solitude of Desolation,
The Wilderness of Death. And as before
Of sundry scented woods along the shore
A shallop he devised to carry them
Over the waters whither foot nor eye
Should ever follow them, he thought—so now
Of sere wood strewn about the plain of Death,
A raft to bear them through the wave of Fire
Into Annihilation, he devised,   (94)
Gather'd, and built; and, firing with a Torch,
Into the central flame ABSÁL and He
Sprung hand in hand exulting. But the SAGE
In secret all had order'd; and the Flame,
Directed by his self-fulfilling WILL,
Devouring Her to ashes, left untouch'd
SALÁMÁN—all the baser metal burn'd,
And to itself the authentic Gold return'd.

SALÁMÁN AND ABSÁL.

PART III.

FROM the Beginning such has been the Fate
Of Man, whose very clay was soak'd in tears.
For when at first of common Earth they took,
And moulded to the stature of the Soul,
For Forty days, full Forty days, the cloud
Of Heav'n wept over him from head to foot:
And when the Forty days had passed to Night,
The Sunshine of one solitary day
Look'd out of Heav'n to dry the weeping clay.[1]
And though that sunshine in the long arrear
   Of darkness on the breathless image rose,
   Yet with the Living, every wise man knows
Such consummation scarcely shall be here!

SALÁMÁN fired the pile; and in the flame
That, passing him, consumed ABSÁL like straw,
Died his Divided Self, his Individual
Surviv'd, and, like a living Soul from which
The Body falls, strange, naked, and alone.
Then rose his cry to Heaven—his eyelashes
(96) Wept blood—his sighs stood like a smoke in Heaven,
And Morning rent her garment at his anguish.

[1] *Some such Legend is quoted by De Sacy and D'Herbelot from some
commentaries on the Kurán.*

And when Night came, that drew the pen across
The written woes of Day for all but him,
Crouch'd in a lonely corner of the house,
He seem'd to feel about him in the dark
For one who was not, and whom no fond word
Could summon from the Void in which she lay.

And so the Wise One found him where he sate
Bow'd down alone in darkness; and once more
Made the long-silent voice of Reason sound
In the deserted Palace of his Soul;
Until SALÁMÁN lifted up his head
To bow beneath the Master; sweet it seem'd,
Sweeping the chaff and litter from his own,
To be the very dust of Wisdom's door,
Slave of the Firmán of the Lord of Life,
Who pour'd the wine of Wisdom in his cup,
Who laid the dew of Peace upon his lips;
Yea, wrought by Miracle in his behalf.
For when old Love return'd to Memory,
And broke in passion from his lips, THE SAGE,
Under whose waxing WILL Existence rose
From Nothing, and, relaxing, waned again,
Raising a Fantom Image of ABSÁL,
Set it awhile before SALÁMÁN's eyes,   (97)
Till, having sow'd the seed of comfort there,

SALÁMÁN AND ABSÁL.

It went again down to Annihilation.
But ever, as the Fantom past away,
THE SAGE would tell of a Celestial Love;
"ZUHRAH," [1] he said, "ZUHRAH, compared with whom
" That brightest star that bears her name in Heav'n
" Was but a winking taper; and Absál,
" Queen-star of Beauties in this world below,
" But her distorted image in the stream
" Of fleeting Matter; and all Eloquence,
" And Soul-enchaining harmonies of Song,
" A far-off echo of that Harp in Heav'n
" Which Dervish-dances to her harmony."

SALÁMÁN listen'd, and inclin'd—again
Entreated, inclination ever grew;
Until THE SAGE beholding in his Soul
The SPIRIT [2] quicken, so effectually
With ZUHRAH wrought, that she reveal'd herself
In her pure lustre to SALÁMÁN's Soul,
And blotting ABSÁL's Image from his breast,
There reign'd instead. Celestial Beauty seen,
(98) He left the Earthly; and, once come to know
Eternal Love, the Mortal he let go.

[1] "ZUHRAH." *The Planetary and Celestial Venus.*
[2] "Maaní." *The Mystical pass-word of the Súfís, to express the transcendental New Birth of the Soul.*

THE Crown of Empire how supreme a lot!
The Sultan's Throne how lofty! Yea, but not
For All—None but the Heaven-ward foot may dare
To mount—The head that touches Heaven to wear!

When the Beloved of Royal augury
Was rescued from the bondage of ABSÁL,
Then he arose, and shaking off the dust
Of that lost travel, girded up his heart,
And look'd with undefiléd robe to Heaven.
Then was his Head worthy to wear the Crown,
His Foot to mount the Throne. And then THE SHÁH
From all the quarters of his World-wide realm
Summon'd all those who under Him the ring
Of Empire wore, King, Counsellor, Amír;
Of whom not one but to SALÁMÁN did
Obeisance, and lifted up his neck
To yoke it under His supremacy.
Then THE SHÁH crown'd him with the Golden Crown,
And set the Golden Throne beneath his feet,
And over all the heads of the Assembly,   (99)
And in the ears of all, his Jewel-word
With the Diamond of Wisdom cut, and said:—

"My Son,[1] the Kingdom of the World is not

" Eternal, nor the sum of right desire;

" Make thou the Law reveal'd of God thy Law,

" The voice of Intellect Divine within

" Interpreter; and considering TO-DAY

" TO-MORROW's Seed-field, ere That come to bear,

" Sow with the harvest of Eternity.

" And, as all Work, and, most of all, the Work

" That Kings are born to, wisely should be wrought,

" Where doubtful of thine own sufficiency,

" Ever, as I have done, consult the Wise.

" Turn not thy face away from the Old ways,

" That were the canon of the Kings of Old;

" Nor cloud with Tyranny the glass of Justice:

(100) " By Mercy rather to right Order turn

" Confusion, and Disloyalty to Love.

" In thy provision for the Realm's estate,

" And for the Honour that becomes a King,

" Drain not thy People's purse—the Tyranny

" Which Thee enriches at thy Subject's cost,

" Awhile shall make thee strong; but in the end

" Shall bow thy neck beneath thy People's hate,

" And lead thee with the Robber down to Hell.

[1] One sees Jámí taking advantage of his Allegorical Sháh to read a lesson to the Living—whose ears Advice, unlike Praise, scarce ever reached, unless obliquely and by Fable. The Warning (and doubtless with good reason) is principally aimed at the Minister.

" Thou art a Shepherd, and thy Flock the People,

" To help and save, not ravage and destroy;

" For which is for the other, Flock or Shepherd?

" And join with thee True men to keep the Flock—

" Dogs, if you will—but trusty—head in leash,

" Whose teeth are for the Wolf, not for the Lamb,

" And least of all the Wolf's accomplices.

" For Sháhs must have Vizyrs—but be they Wise

" And Trusty—knowing well the Realm's estate—

" Knowing how far to Sháh and Subject bound

" On either hand—not by extortion, nor

" By usury wrung from the People's purse,

" Feeding their Master, and themselves (with whom

" Enough is apt enough to make rebel)

" To such a surfeit feeding as feeds Hell.

" Proper in soul and body be they—pitiful

" To Poverty—hospitable to the Saint—

" Their sweet Access a salve to wounded Hearts; *(101)*

" Their Wrath a sword against Iniquity,

" But at thy bidding only to be drawn;

" Whose Ministers they are, to bring thee in

" Report of Good or Evil through the Realm:

  " Which to confirm with thine immediate Eye,

" And least of all, remember—least of all,

" Suffering Accuser also to be Judge,

  " By surest steps up-builds Prosperity."

MEANING OF THE STORY.

UNDER the leaf of many a Fable lies
The Truth for those who look for it; of this
If thou wouldst look behind and find the Fruit,
(To which the Wiser hand hath found his way)
Have thy desire—No Tale of ME and THEE,
Though I and THOU be its Interpreters.[1]
What signifies THE SHÁH? and what THE SAGE?
And what SALÁMÁN not of Woman born?
Who was ABSÁL who drew him to Desire?
And what the KINGDOM that awaited him
When he had drawn his Garment from her hand?
What means THAT SEA? And what that FIERY PILE?
And what that Heavenly ZUHRAH who at last
Clear'd ABSÁL from the Mirror of his Soul?
Listen to me, and you shall understand
The Word that Lover wrote along the sand.[2]

---

(103) THE incomparable Creator, when this World
He did create, created first of all

[1] *The Story is of* Generals, *though enacted by* Particulars.
[2] *See page 60.*

[100]

The FIRST INTELLIGENCE [1]—First of a Chain
Of Ten Intelligences, of which the Last
Sole Agent is in this our Universe,
ACTIVE INTELLIGENCE so call'd; The One
Distributer of Evil and of Good,
Of Joy and Sorrow. Himself apart from MATTER,   *(104)*
In Essence and in Energy—He yet
Hath fashion'd all that is—Material Form,
And Spiritual, all from HIM—by HIM
Directed all, and in his Bounty drown'd.
Therefore is He that Firmán-issuing SHÁH
To whom the World was subject. But because
What He distributes to the Universe
  Another and a Higher Power supplies,

[1] *"These Ten Intelligences are only another Form of the Gnostic
Dæmones. The Gnostics held that Matter and Spirit could have no
Intercourse—they were, as it were, incommensurate. How, then,
granting this premise, was Creation possible? Their answer was a
kind of gradual Elimination. God, the 'Actus Purus,' created an
Aeon; this Aeon created a Second; and so on, until the Tenth Aeon
was sufficiently Material (as the Ten were in a continually descending
Series) to affect Matter, and so cause the Creation by giving to Mat-
ter the Spiritual Form.*
  *"Similarly we have in Sufiism these Ten Intelligences in a corre-
sponding Series, and for the same End.*
  *"There are Ten Intelligences, and Nine Heavenly Spheres, of which
the Ninth is the Uppermost Heaven, appropriated to the First Intel-
ligence; the Eighth, that of the Zodiac, to the Second; the Seventh,
Saturn, to the Third; the Sixth, Jupiter, to the Fourth; the Fifth,
Mars, to the Fifth; the Fourth, The Sun, to the Sixth; the Third,
Venus, to the Seventh; the Second, Mercury, to the Eighth; the First,
the Moon, to the Ninth; and* THE EARTH *is the peculiar Sphere of
the Tenth, or lowest Intelligence, called* THE ACTIVE.*" E. B. C.—v.
Appendix.*

[101   ]

Therefore all those who comprehend aright,
That Higher in THE SAGE will recognise.
HIS the PRIME SPIRIT that, spontaneously
Projected by the TENTH INTELLIGENCE,
Was from no Womb of MATTER reproduced
A special Essence called THE SOUL OF MAN;
A Child of Heaven, in raiment unbeshamed
Of Sensual taint, and so SALÁMÁN named.

And who ABSÁL?—The Sense-adoring Body,
Slave to the Blood and Sense—through whom THE SOUL,
Although the Body's very Life it be,
Doth yet imbibe the knowledge and delight
Of things of SENSE; and these in such a bond
United as GOD only can divide,
As Lovers in this Tale are signified.

(105) And what the Flood on which they sail'd, with those
Fantastic creatures peopled; and that Isle
In which their Paradise awhile they made,
And thought, for ever?—That false Paradise
Amid the fluctuating Waters found
Of Sensual passion, in whose bosom lies
A world of Being from the light of God
Deep as in unsubsiding Deluge drown'd.

And why was it that ABSÁL in that Isle
So soon deceived in her Delight, and He
Fell short of his Desire?—that was to show
How soon the Senses of their Passion tire,
And in a surfeit of themselves expire.

And what the turning of SALÁMÁN's Heart
Back to the SHÁH, and to the throne of Might
And Glory yearning?—What but the return
Of the lost SOUL to his true Parentage,
And back from Carnal error looking up
Repentant to his Intellectual Right.

And when the Man between his living Shame
Distracted, and the Love that would not die,
Fled once again—what meant that second Flight
Into the Desert, and that Pile of Fire
On which he fain his Passion with Himself   (106)
Would immolate?—That was the Discipline
To which the living Man himself devotes,
Till all the Sensual dross be scorcht away,
And, to its pure integrity return'd,
His Soul alone survives. But forasmuch
As from a darling Passion so divorced
The wound will open and will bleed anew,
Therefore THE SAGE would ever and anon

Raise up and set before Salámán's eyes
That Fantom of the past; but evermore
Revealing one Diviner, till his Soul
She fill'd, and blotted out the Mortal Love.
For what is ZUHRAH?—What but that Divine
Original, of which the Soul of Man
Darkly possest, by that fierce Discipline
At last he disengages from the Dust,
And flinging off the baser rags of Sense,
And all in Intellectual Light arrayed,
As Conqueror and King he mounts the Throne,
And wears the Crown of Human Glory—Whence,
Throne over Throne surmounting, he shall reign
One with the LAST and FIRST INTELLIGENCE.

---

(107) This is the meaning of this Mystery,
Which to know wholly ponder in thy Heart,
Till all its ancient Secret be enlarged.
Enough—The written Summary I close,
And set my Seal—

THE
TRUTH
GOD ONLY
KNOWS.

APPENDIX.

"To thy Harím Dividuality
"No entrance finds," &c. (p. 56.)

This Súfí Identification with Deity (further illustrated in the Story of Salámán's first flight) is shadowed in a Parable of Jelálud-dín, of which here is an outline. "One knocked at the Beloved's Door; and a Voice asked from within, 'Who is there?' and he answered, 'It is I.' Then the Voice said, 'This House will not hold Me and Thee.' And the Door was not opened. Then went the Lover into the Desert, and fasted and prayed in Solitude. And after a Year he returned, and knocked again at the Door. And again the Voice asked, 'Who is there?' and he said, 'It is Thyself!'—and the Door was opened to him."

"O darling of the soul of Iflatún
"To whom with all his school Aristo bows." (p. 63.)

Some Traveller in the East—Professor Eastwick, I think—tells us that in endeavouring to explain to an Eastern Cook the nature of an *Irish Stew*, the man said he knew well enough about *"Aristo."* *"Iflatún"* might almost as well have been taken for *"Vol-au-vent."*

"Like Noah's, puff'd with Insolence and Pride," &c. (p. 64.)

In the Kurán God engages to save Noah and his Family,—meaning all who believed in the Warning. One of Noah's Sons | (Canaan (109) or Ham, some think) would not believe. "And the Ark swam with them between waves like Mountains, and Noah called up to his Son, who was separated from him, saying, 'Embark with us, my Son, and stay not with the Unbelievers.' He answered, 'I will get on a Mountain, which will secure me from the Water.' Noah replied, 'There is no security this Day from the Decree of God, except for him on whom he shall have Mercy.' And a Wave passed between them, and he became one of those who were drowned. And it was said, 'O Earth, swallow up thy waters, and Thou, O Heaven, withhold

APPENDIX.

thy Rain!' And immediately the Water abated, and the Decree was
fulfilled, and the Ark rested on the Mountain Al Judi; and it was
said, 'Away with the ungodly People!' And Noah called upon his
Lord, and said, 'O Lord, verily my Son is of my Family, and thy
Promise is True; for Thou art the most just of those who exercise
Judgment.' God answered, 'O Noah, verily he is not of thy Family:
this intercession of thine for him is not a righteous work.'"—*Sale's
Kurán,* vol. ii. p. 21.

"Finer than any Bridal-puppet, which
"To prove another's Love a Woman sends," &c. (p. 69.)

In Atkinson's version of the "Kitábi Kulsúm Naneh" [c. xii.] we
find among other Ceremonials and Proprieties of which the Book
treats, that when a Woman wished to ascertain another's Love, she
sent a Doll on a Tray with flowers and sweetmeats, and judged how
far her affection was reciprocated by the Doll's being returned to her
drest in a Robe of Honour, or in Black. The same Book also tells of
(110) *two* Dolls—Bride and Bridegroom, | I suppose—being used on such
occasions; the test of Affection being whether the one sent were returned with or without its Fellow.

"The Royal Game of Chúgán." (p. 71.)

For centuries the Royal Game of Persia, and adopted (Ouseley
thinks) under varying modifications of name and practice by other
nations, was played by Horsemen, who, suitably habited, and armed
with semicircular-headed Bats or Sticks, strove to drive a Ball
through a Goal of upright Pillars. (See Frontispiece.) We may
call it "Horse-hockey," as heretofore played by young Englishmen
in the Maidán of Calcutta, and other Indian cities, I believe, and now
in England itself under the name of Polo.

The Frontispiece to this version of the Poem is accurately copied
from an Engraving in Sir William's Book, which he says (and those
who care to look into the Bodleian [1] for it may see), is "accurately
copied from a very beautiful Persian MS., containing the works of
Háfiz, transcribed in the year 956 of the Hijrah, 1549 of Christ;
the MS. is in my own Collection. This Delineation exhibits two
Horsemen contending for the Ball; their short Jackets seem peculiarly
adapted to this Sport; we see the Míl, or Goals; Servants attend
on Foot, holding Chúgáns in readiness for other Persons who may

[1] MS. Ouseley 20.

APPENDIX.

join in the Amusement, or to supply the place of any that may be broken. A young Prince (as his PARR, or Feather, would indicate) receives on his Entrance into the MEIDÁN, or Place of Exercise, a CHÚGÁN from the hands of a bearded Man, very plainly dressed; yet, as an intelligent Painter at Ispahan assured me, (and as appears | from other Miniatures in the same Book) this Bearded Figure is de- *(111)* signed to represent Háfiz himself," &c.

The Persian legend at the Top Corner is the Verse from Háfiz which the Drawing illustrates:

Shahsuvára khúsh bemeidán ámedy gúy bezann.

THE MUEZZÍN'S CRY. (p. 82.)

I am informed by a distinguished Arabic Scholar that the proper Cry of the Muezzín is, with some slight local variations, such as he heard it at Cairo and Damascus:

Allah Akbar, Allah Akbar;
Allah Akbar, Allah Akbar;
Ishhad lá allah illá 'llah;
Ishhad lá allah illá 'llah;
Ishhad lá allah illá 'llah;
Ishhad Muhammad rasulúhu;
Ishhad Muhammad rasulúhu;
Ishhad Muhammad rasulúhu;
Hayá 'alá 's-salát, Hayá 'alá 's-salát,
Inna 's-salát, khair min an-naum.

"God is great" *(four times);* "Confess that there is no God but God" *(three times);* "Confess that Muhammad is the prophet of God" *(three times);* "Come to Prayer, Come to Prayer, for Prayer is better than Sleep."
[A more accurate account will be found in Lane's Modern Egyptians.]

THE GARDEN OF IRAM. (p. 86.)   *(112)*

"Here Iram-Garden seem'd in secresy
"Blowing the rosebud of its Revelation."

"Mahomet," says Sir W. Jones, "in the Chapter of The Morning, towards the end of his Alcoran, mentions a Garden called 'Irem,' which is no less celebrated by the Asiatic Poets than that of the Hes-

APPENDIX.

perides by the Greeks. It was planted, as the Commentators say, by a king named Shedád,"—deep in the Sands of Arabia Felix,—"and was once seen by an Arabian who wandered far into the Desert in search of a lost Camel."

THE TEN INTELLIGENCES. (p. 101.)

A curious parallel to this doctrine is quoted by Mr. Morley (Critical Miscellanies, Series II., p. 318), from so anti-gnostic a Doctor as Paley, in Ch. III. of his Natural Theology.

"As we have said, therefore, God prescribes limits to his power, that he may let in the exercise, and thereby exhibit demonstrations, of his wisdom. For then—*i. e.,* such laws and limitations being laid down, it is as though some Being should have fixed certain rules; and, if we may so speak, provided certain materials; and, afterwards, have committed to some other Being, out of these materials, and in subordination to these rules, the task of drawing forth a Creation; a supposition which evidently leaves room, and induces indeed a necessity, for contrivance. Nay, there may be many such Agents, and many ranks of these. We do not advance this as a doctrine either of philosophy or religion; but we say that the subject may be safely represented under this view; because the Deity, acting himself by general laws, will have the same consequence upon our reasoning, as if he had prescribed these laws to another."

[NOTE. The pagination in the margins is that of the Third edition, 1879.]

EXTRACTS FROM FITZGERALD'S LETTERS RELATING TO "EUPHRANOR" THIRD EDITION.

To C. E. Norton.

Woodbridge, August 5, 1881.

. . . *It has all made me think of a very little Dialogue I once wrote on the matter, thirty years ago and more, which I really think of putting into shape again: and, if I do, will send it to you, by way of picture of what our Cambridge was in what I think were better days than now.* . . .

To Hallam Tennyson.

Woodbridge, May 28, [1882].

My dear Hallam:

I believe I ought to be ashamed of reviving the little thing which accompanies this Letter. My excuse must be that I have often been askt for a copy when I had no more to give; and a visit to Cambridge last summer, to the old familiar places, if not faces, made me take it up once more and turn it into what you now see. I should certainly not send a copy to you, or yours, but for what relates to your Father in it. He did not object, so far as I know, to what I said of him, though not by name, in a former Edition; but there is more of him in this, though still not by name, nor, as you see, intended for Publication. All of this you can read to him, if you please, at pp. 25 and 56. I do not ask him to say that he approves of what is said, or meant to be said, in his honour; and I only ask you to tell me if he disapproves of its going any further. I owed you a letter in return for the kind one you sent me; and, if I do not hear from you to the contrary, I shall take silence, if not for consent, at least not for prohibition. I really did, and do, wish my first, which is also my last, little work to record, for a few years at least, my love and admiration of that dear old Fellow, my old Friend.

To R. C. Trench.

July 3, 1861.

. . . What your Mother says of the Dresden Madonna reminds me of what Tennyson once said: that the Attitude of The Child was that of a Man: but perhaps not the less right for all that. As to the Countenance, he said that scarce any Man's Face could look so grave and rapt as a Baby's could at times. He once said of his own Child's, 'He was a whole hour this morning worshipping the Sunshine playing on the Bedpost.' **

To C. E. Norton.

Woodbridge, June 9, '82.

I told you, I think, but I scarce know when, that I would send you a very little Tract of mine written forty

* See page 140.

*years ago; and reformed into its present shape in conse-
quence of copies being askt for when I had none to give.
So a few days at Cambridge last Summer, among the
old places, though not faces, set me off. 'Et voilà qui est
fait,' and posted to you along with this Letter, together
with a Copy for Professor Goodwin. The first and last
of my little works: and I do think a pretty specimen of
'chisell'd Cherry-stone.' Having which opinion myself,
I more than ever deprecate any word of praise from any
to whom I send it. Nay, I even assume beforehand that
you will like it too: and Professor Goodwin also (so do
not let him write): as my little tribute to my own old
Cambridge sent to you in your new. I think I shall send
it to Mr. Lowell too. So you see that I need no compliment, no, nor even acknowledgment of it. . . .*

EUPHRANOR

EUPHRANOR,

𝕬 𝔐𝔞𝔶-𝔇𝔞𝔶 𝔠𝔬𝔫𝔳𝔢𝔯𝔰𝔞𝔱𝔦𝔬𝔫 𝔞𝔱 𝔠𝔞𝔪𝔟𝔯𝔦𝔡𝔤𝔢.

' 'TIS FORTY YEARS SINCE.

EUPHRANOR.

DURING the time of my pretending to practise Medicine at Cambridge, I was aroused, one fine forenoon of May, by the sound of some one coming up my staircase, two or three steps at a time it seemed to me; then, directly after, a smart rapping at the door; and, before I could say, " Come in," Euphranor had opened it, and, striding up to me, seized my arm with his usual eagerness, and told me I must go out with him—" It was such a day—sun shining—breeze blowing—hedges and trees in full leaf.—He had been to Chesterton, (he said,) and pull'd back with a man who now left him in the lurch; and I must take his place." I told him what a poor hand at the oar I was, and, such walnut-shells as these Cambridge boats were, I was sure a strong fellow like him must rejoice in getting a whole Eight-oar to himself once in a while. He laughed, and said, " The pace, the pace was the thing— However, that was all nothing, but—in short, I must go with him, whether for a row, or a walk in the fields, or a game of Billiards at Chesterton—whatever I liked—only go I must." After a little more banter, about some possible Patients, I got up;|closed some very weary medi- (2) cal Treatise I was reading; on with coat and hat; and in three minutes we had run downstairs, out into the open air; where both of us calling out together " What a day! " it was, we struck out briskly for the old Wooden Bridge, where Euphranor said his boat was lying.

" By-the-by," said I, as we went along, " it would be
a charity to knock up poor Lexilogus, and carry him
along with us."

Not much of a charity, Euphranor thought—Lexilogus would so much rather be left with his books. Which
I declared was the very reason he should be taken from
them; and Euphranor, who was quite good-humour'd,
and wish'd Lexilogus all well (for we were all three
Yorkshiremen, whose families lived no great distance
asunder), easily consented. So, without more ado, we
turn'd into Trinity Great gate, and round by the right
up a staircase to the attic where Lexilogus kept.

The door was *sported,* as they say, but I knew he must
be within; so, using the privilege of an old friend, I
shouted to him through the letter-slit. Presently we
heard the sound of books falling, and soon after Lexilogus' thin, pale, and spectacled face appear'd at the half-
open'd door. He was always glad to see me, I believe,
howsoever I disturb'd him; and he smiled as he laid his
hand in mine, rather than return'd its pressure: working
hard, as he was, poor fellow, for a Fellowship that should
repay all the expense of sending him to College.

The tea-things were still on the table, and I asked him
(though I knew well enough) if he were so fashionable
as only just to have breakfasted?

" Oh—long ago—directly after morning Chapel."

(3)   I then told him he must put his books away, and come
out on the river with Euphranor and myself.

" He could not possibly," he thought;—" not so early,

at least—preparing for some Examination, or course of Lectures——"

" Come, come, my good fellow," said Euphranor, " that is the very reason, says the Doctor; and he will have his way. So make haste."

I then told him (what I then suddenly remember'd) that, beside other reasons, his old Aunt, a Cambridge tradesman's widow whom I attended, and whom Lexilogus help'd to support out of his own little savings, wanted to see him on some business. He should go with us to Chesterton, where she lodged; visit her while Euphranor and I play'd a game or two of Billiards at the Inn; and afterwards (for I knew how little of an oars-man he was) we would all three take a good stretch into the Fields together.

He supposed " we should be back in good time "; about which I would make no condition; and he then resign'd himself to Destiny. While he was busy changing and brushing his clothes, Euphranor, who had walk'd somewhat impatiently about the room, looking now at the books, and now through the window at some white pigeons wheeling about in the clear sky, went up to the mantelpiece and call'd out, " What a fine new pair of screens Lexilogus had got! the present, doubtless, of some fair Lady."

Lexilogus said they were a present from his sister on his birthday; and coming up to me, brush in hand, asked if I recognised the views represented on them?

" Quite well, quite well," I said—" the old Church—

the Yew tree — the Parsonage — one cannot mistake them."

" And were they not beautifully done? "

(4) And I answer'd without hesitation, " they were; " for I knew the girl who had painted them, and that (whatever they might be in point of Art) a still finer spirit had guided her hand.

At last, after a little hesitation as to whether he should wear cap and gown, (which I decided he should, for this time only, *not*,) Lexilogus was ready: and calling out on the staircase to some invisible Bed-maker, that his books should not be meddled with, we ran downstairs, crossed the Great Court—through the Screens, as they are call'd, perpetually travers'd by Gyp, Cook, Bed-maker, and redolent of perpetual Dinner;—and so, through the cloisters of Neville's Court, out upon the open green before the Library. The sun shone broad on the new-shaven expanse of grass, while holiday-seeming people saunter'd along the River-side, and under the trees, now flourishing in freshest green—the Chestnut especially in full fan, and leaning down his white cones over the sluggish current, which seem'd indeed fitter for the slow merchandise of coal, than to wash the walls and flow through the groves of Academe.

We now consider'd that we had miss'd our proper point of embarkation; but this was easily set right at a slight expense of College propriety. Euphranor calling out to some one who had his boat in charge along with others by the wooden bridge, we descended the grassy slope,

stepp'd in, with due caution on the part of Lexilogus and
myself, and settled the order of our voyage. Euphranor
and I were to pull, and Lexilogus (as I at first proposed)
to steer. But seeing he was somewhat shy of meddling
in the matter, I agreed to take all the blame of my own
awkwardness on myself.

"And just take care of this, will you, Lexilogus?" said
|Euphranor, handing him a book which fell out of the (5)
pocket of the coat he was taking off.

" Oh, books, books!" I exclaimed. " I thought we were
to steer clear of them, at any rate. Now we shall have
Lexilogus reading all the way, instead of looking about
him, and inhaling the fresh air unalloy'd. What is it—
Greek, Algebra, German, or what?"

" None of these, however," Euphranor said, " but only
Digby's Godefridus "; and then asking me whether I was
ready, and I calling out, " Ay, ay, Sir," our oars plash'd
in the water. Safe through the main arch of Trinity
bridge, we shot past the Library, I exerting myself so
strenuously (as bad rowers are apt to do), that I almost
drove the boat upon a very unobtrusive angle of the
College buildings. This danger past, however, we got
on better; Euphranor often looking behind him to anticipate our way; and counteracting with his experienced
oar the many misdirections of mine. Amid all this, he
had leisure to ask me if I knew those same Digby books?

" Some of them," I told him—" the ' Broad Stone of
Honour,' for one; indeed I had the first Protestant edition of it, now very rare."

" But not so good as the enlarged Catholic," said
Euphranor, " of which this Godefridus is part."

" Perhaps not," I replied; " but then, on the other hand,
not so Catholic; which you and Lexilogus will agree with
me is much in its favour."

Which I said slyly, because of Euphranor's being
rather taken with the Oxford doctrine just then coming
into vogue.

" You cannot forgive him that," said he.

" Nay, nay," said I, " one can forgive a true man anything."

(6) And then Euphranor ask'd me, " Did I not remember
Digby himself at College?—perhaps know him? "

"Not *that,*" I answer'd, but remember'd him very well.
" A grand, swarthy Fellow, who might have stept out of
the canvas of some knightly portrait in his Father's hall
—perhaps the living image of one sleeping under some
cross-legg'd Effigies in the Church."

" And, Hare says, really the Knight at heart that he
represented in his Books."

" At least," I answered, " he pull'd a very good stroke
on the river, where I am now labouring so awkwardly."

In which and other such talk, interrupted by the little
accidents of our voyage, we had threaded our way through
the closely-packt barges at Magdalen; through the Locks;
and so for a pull of three or four miles down the river and
back again to the Ferry; where we surrender'd our boat,
and footed it over the fields to Chesterton, at whose
Church we came just as its quiet chimes were preluding

Twelve o'clock. Close by was the humble house whither Lexilogus was bound. I look'd in for a moment at the old lady, and left him with her, privately desiring him to join us as soon as he could at the Three Tuns Inn, which I preferr'd to any younger rival, because of the many pleasant hours I had spent there in my own College days, some twenty years ago.

When Euphranor and I got there, we found all the tables occupied; but one, as usual, would be at our service before long. Meanwhile, ordering some light ale after us, we went into the Bowling-green, with its Lilac bushes now in full bloom and full odour; and there we found, sitting alone upon a bench, Lycion, with a cigar in his mouth, and rolling the bowls about lazily with his foot.

" What! Lycion! and all alone! " I call'd out.

He nodded to us both—waiting, he said, till some men (7) had finish'd a pool of billiards upstairs—a great bore—for it was only just begun! and one of the fellows " a man I particularly detest."

" Come and console yourself with some ale, then," said I. " Are you ever foolish enough to go pulling on the river, as we have been doing? "

" Not very often in hot weather; he did not see the use," he said, " of perspiring to no purpose."

" Just so," replied I, " though Euphranor has not turn'd a hair, you see, owing to the good condition he is in. But here comes our liquor; and ' Sweet is Pleasure after Pain,' at any rate."

We then sat down in one of those little arbours cut into

the Lilac bushes round the Bowling-green; and while Euphranor and I were quaffing each a glass of Home-brew'd, Lycion took up the volume of Digby, which Euphranor had laid on the table.

" Ah, Lycion," said Euphranor, putting down his glass, " there is one would have put you up to a longer and stronger pull than we have had to-day?"

" Chivalry——" said Lycion, glancing carelessly over the leaves; " Don't you remember," — addressing me — " what an absurd thing that Eglinton Tournament was? What a complete failure! There was the Queen of Beauty on her throne—Lady Seymour—who alone of all the whole affair was *not* a sham—and the Heralds, and the Knights in full Armour on their horses—they had been practising for months, I believe—but unluckily, at the very moment of Onset, the rain began, and the Knights threw down their lances, and put up their um-brellas."

I laugh'd, and said I remembered something like it *(8)* |had occurr'd, though not to that umbrella-point, which I thought was a theatrical, or Louis Philippe Burlesque on the affair. And I asked Euphranor " what he had to say in defence of the Tournament "?

" Nothing at all," he replied. " It *was* a silly thing, and fit to be laughed at for the very reason that it *was* a sham, as Lycion says. As Digby himself tells us," he went on, taking the Book, and rapidly turning over the leaves—" Here it is "—and he read: " ' The error that leads men to doubt of this first proposition '—that is, you

know, that Chivalry is not a thing past, but, like all things
of Beauty, eternal—' the error that leads men to doubt
of this first proposition consists of their supposing that
Tournaments, and steel Panoply, and Coat arms, and
Aristocratic institutions, are essential to Chivalry;
whereas, these are, in fact, only accidental attendants
upon it, subject to the influence of Time, which changes
all such things.' "

" I suppose," said Lycion, " your man—whatever his
name is—would carry us back to the days of King Arthur,
and the Seven Champions, whenever they were—that one
used to read about when a Child? I thought Don Quixote had put an end to all that long ago."

" Well, *he,* at any rate," said Euphranor, " did not
depend on fine Accoutrement for his Chivalry."

" Nay," said I, " but did he *not* believe in his rusty
armour—perhaps even the paste-board Visor he fitted to
it—as impregnable as the Cause———"

" And some old Barber's bason as the Helmet of Mam-
brino," interposed Lycion———

" And his poor Rocinante not to be surpass'd by the
Bavieca of the Cid; believed in all this, I say, as really
as in the Windmills and Wine-skins being the Giants and
Sorcerers he was to annihilate? "

" To be sure he did," said Lycion; " but Euphranor's *(9)*
Round-table men—many of them great rascals, I believe
—knew a real Dragon, or Giant—when they met him—
better than Don Quixote."

" Perhaps, however," said I, who saw Euphranor's col-

our rising, "he and Digby would tell us that all such
Giants and Dragons may be taken for Symbols of certain
Forms of Evil which his Knights went about to encoun-
ter and exterminate."

"Of course," said Euphranor, with an indignant snort,
"every Child knows that: then as now to be met with and
put down in whatsoever shapes they appear as long as
Tyranny and Oppression exist."

"Till finally extinguisht, as they crop up, by Euphranor and his Successors," said Lycion.

"Does not Carlyle somewhere talk to us of a 'Chivalry
of Labour'?" said I; "that henceforward not 'Arms and
the Man,' but 'Tools and the Man,' are to furnish the
Epic of the world."

"Oh, well," said Lycion, "if the 'Table-Round' turn
into a Tailor's Board—'Charge, Chester, charge!' say
I—only not exorbitantly for the Coat you provide for
us—which indeed, like true Knights, I believe you should
provide for us gratis."

"Yes, my dear fellow," said I, laughing, "but then
You must not sit idle, smoking your cigar, in the midst
of it; but, as your Ancestors led on mail'd troops at Agincourt, so must you put yourself, shears in hand, at the
head of this Host, and become what Carlyle calls 'a Captain of Industry,' a Master-tailor, leading on a host of
Journeymen to fresh fields and conquests new."

"Besides," said Euphranor, who did not like Carlyle,
(10) |nor relish this sudden descent of his hobby, "surely
Chivalry will never want a good Cause to maintain,

[122]

whether private or public. As Tennyson says, King Arthur, who was carried away wounded to the island valley of Avilion, returns to us in the shape of a ' modern Gentleman ' ;* and, the greater his Power and opportunity, the more demanded of him."

" Which you must bear in mind, Lycion," said I, " if ever you come to legislate for us in your Father's Borough."

" Or out of it, also," said Euphranor, " with something other than the Doctor's Shears at your side; as in case of any National call to Arms."

To this Lycion, however, only turn'd his cigar in his mouth by way of reply, and look'd somewhat superciliously at his Antagonist. And I, who had been looking into the leaves of the Book that Euphranor had left open, said:

" Here we are, as usual, discussing without having yet agreed on the terms we are using. Euphranor has told us, on the word of his Hero, what Chivalry is *not:* let him read us what it *is* that we are talking about."

I then handed him the Book to read to us, while Lycion, lying down on the grass, with his hat over his eyes, composed himself to inattention. And Euphranor read:

" ' Chivalry is only a name for that general Spirit or state of mind, which disposes men to Heroic and Generous actions; and keeps them conversant with all that is Beauti-

* *"Who may be challenged, even in these later days, to no mock Tournament, Lycion, in his Country's defence, and with something other than the Doctor's shears at his side."*—The sentence finishes thus, and the two subsequent paragraphs are omitted in final edition.

ful and Sublime in the Intellectual and Moral world. It
will be found that, in the absence of conservative principles, this Spirit more generally prevails in Youth than
in the later periods of men's lives: and, as the Heroic is
always the earliest age in the history of nations, so Youth,
the first period of human life, may be considered as the
(11) Heroic or|Chivalrous age of each separate Man; and
there are few so unhappy as to have grown up without
having experienced its influence, and having derived the
advantage of being able to enrich their imaginations, and
to soothe their hours of sorrow, with its romantic recol-
lections. The Anglo-Saxons distinguished the period
between Childhood and Manhood by the term 'Cnihthade,'
Knighthood; a term which still continued to indicate the
connexion between Youth and Chivalry, when Knights
were styled 'Children,' as in the historic song beginning

"Childe Rowland to the dark tower came,"

an excellent expression, no doubt; for every Boy and
Youth is, in his mind and sentiments, a Knight, and essentially a Son of Chivalry. Nature is fine in him. Nothing but the circumstance of a singular and most degrad-
ing system of Education can ever totally destroy the
action of this general law. Therefore, as long as there
has been, or shall be, a succession of sweet Springs in
Man's Intellectual World; as long as there have been,
or shall be, Young men to grow up to maturity; and
until all Youthful life shall be dead, and its source with-
ered for ever; so long must there have been, and must

[124]

there continue to be, the spirit of noble Chivalry. To understand therefore this first and, as it were, natural Chivalry, we have only to observe the features of the Youthful age, of which examples surround us. For, as Demipho says of young men:

"Ecce autem similia omnia: omnes congruunt:
Unum cognoris, omnes noris."

Mark the courage of him who is green and fresh in this Old world. Amyntas beheld and dreaded the insolence of the Persians; but not so Alexander, the son of Amyntas, ἄτε|νέος τε ἐὼν, καὶ κακῶν ἀπαθὴς (says Herodotus) (12) οὐδαμῶς ἔτι κατέχειν οἷός τε ἦν. When Jason had related to his companions the conditions imposed by the King, the first impression was that of horror and despondency; till Peleus rose up boldly, and said,

Ὤρη μητιάασθαι ὅ κ' ἔρξομεν· οὐ μὲν ἔολπα
Βουλῆς εἶναι ὄνειαρ, ὅσον τ' ἐπὶ κάρτεϊ χειρῶν.

'If Jason be unwilling to attempt it, I and the rest will undertake the enterprise; for what more can we suffer than death?' And then instantly rose up Telamon and Idas, and the sons of Tyndarus, and Œnides, although

—οὐδέ περ ὅσσον ἐπανθιόωντας ἰούλους
Ἀντέλλων.

But Argus, the Nestor of the party, restrained their impetuous valour.'"

" Scarce the Down upon their lips, you see," (said I,) " Freshmen;—so that you, Euphranor, who are now

[125]

Bachelor of Arts, and whose upper lip at least begins to show the stubble of repeated harvests, are, alas, fast declining from that golden prime of Knighthood, while Lycion here, whose shavings might almost be counted ——"

Here Lycion, who had endured the reading with an occasional yawn, said he wish'd "those fellows upstairs would finish their pool."

"And see again," continued I, taking the book from Euphranor's hands—" after telling us that Chivalry is mainly but another name for Youth, Digby proceeds to define more particularly what *that* is—' It is a remark of Lord Bacon, that " for the Moral part, Youth will have the pre-eminence, as Age hath for the Politic; " and this has always been the opinion which is allied to that other belief, that the Heroic (the Homeric age) was the most *(13)* |Virtuous age of Greece. When Demosthenes is desirous of expressing any great and generous sentiment, he uses the term νεανικὸν φρόνημα '—and by the way," added I, looking up parenthetically from the book, " the Persians, I am told, employ the same word for Youth and Courage—' and it is the saying of Plautus, when surprise is evinced at the Benevolence of an old man, " Benignitas hujus ut Adolescentuli est." There is no difference, says the Philosopher, between Youthful Age and Youthful Character; and what this is cannot be better evinced than in the very words of Aristotle: " The Young are ardent in Desire, and what they do is from Affection; they are tractable and delicate; they earnestly desire and are quickly

[126]

appeased; their wishes are intense, without comprehend-
ing much, as the thirst and hunger of the weary; they are
passionate and hasty, and liable to be surprised by anger;
for being ambitious of Honour, they cannot endure to be
despised, but are indignant when they suffer injustice;
they love Honour, but still more Victory; for Youth
desires superiority, and victory is superiority, and both of
these they love more than Riches; for as to these, of all
things, they care for them the least. They are not of
corrupt manners, but are Innocent, from not having
beheld much wickedness; and they are credulous, from
having been seldom deceived; and Sanguine in hope, for,
like persons who are drunk with wine, they are inflamed
by nature, and from their having had but little experience
of Fortune. And they live by Hope, for Hope is of the
future, but Memory is of the past, and to Youth the
Future is everything, the Past but little; they hope all
things, and remember nothing: and it is easy to deceive
them, for the reasons which have been given; for they are
willing to hope, and are full of Courage, being passionate
|and hasty, of which tempers it is the nature of one not *(14)*
to fear, and of the other to inspire confidence; and they
are easily put to Shame, for they have no resources to
set aside the precepts which they have learned: and they
have lofty souls, for they have never been disgraced or
brought low; and they are unacquainted with Necessity;
they prefer Honour to Advantage, Virtue to Expediency; for they live by Affection rather than by Reason,
and Reason is concerned with Expediency, but Affec-

tion with Honour: and they are warm friends and hearty
companions, more than other men, because they delight
in Fellowship, and judge of nothing by Utility, and
therefore not their friends; and they chiefly err in doing
all things over much, for they keep no medium. They
love much, and they dislike much, and so in everything,
and this arises from their idea that they know everything.
And their faults consist more in Insolence than in actual
wrong; and they are full of Mercy, because they regard
all men as good, and more virtuous than they are; for they
measure others by their own Innocence; so that they suppose every man suffers wrongfully." ' So that Lycion,
you see," said I, looking up from the book, and tapping
on the top of his hat, " is, in virtue of his eighteen Sum-
mers only, a Knight of Nature's own dubbing—yes, and
here we have a list of the very qualities which constitute
him one of the Order. And all the time he is pretending
to be careless, indolent, and worldly, he is really bursting
with suppressed Energy, Generosity, and Devotion."

" I did not try to understand your English any more
than your Greek," said Lycion; " but if I can't help being
the very fine Fellow whom I think you were reading
about, why, I want to know what is the use of writing
books about it for my edification."

(15)   " O yes, my dear fellow," said I, " it is like giving you
an Inventory of your goods, which else you lose, or even
fling away, in your march to Manhood—which you are
so eager to reach. Only to repent when gotten there; for
I see Digby goes on—' What is termed *Entering the*

[128]

World'—which Manhood of course must do—' assuming its Principles and Maxims'—which usually follows—' is nothing else but departing into those regions to which the souls of the Homeric Heroes went sorrowing—

"'ὃν πότμον γοόωσα, λιποῦσ' ἀνδροτῆτα καὶ ἥβην.'"

" Ah, you remember," said Euphranor, " how Lamb's friend, looking upon the Eton Boys in their Cricket-field, sighed ' to think of so many fine Lads so soon turning into frivolous Members of Parliament!' "

" But why ' frivolous '? " said Lycion.

" Ay, why ' frivolous '? " echoed I, " when entering on the Field where Euphranor tells us, their Knightly service may be call'd into action."

" Perhaps," said Euphranor, " entering before sufficiently equipp'd for that part of their calling."

" Well," said Lycion, " the Laws of England determine otherwise, and that is enough for me, and, I suppose, for her, whatever your ancient or modern pedants say to the contrary."

" You mean," said I, " in settling Twenty-one as the Age of ' Discretion,' sufficient to manage, not your own affairs only, but those of the Nation also? "

The hat nodded.

" Not yet, perhaps, accepted for a Parliamentary Knight complete," said I, " so much as Squire to some more experienced, if not more valiant, Leader. Only providing that Neoptolemus do not fall into the hands of a too politic|Ulysses, and under him lose that generous *(16)*

[129]

Moral, whose Inventory is otherwise apt to get lost among
the benches of St. Stephen's—in spite of preliminary
Prayer."

" Aristotle's Master, I think," added Euphranor, with
some mock gravity, " would not allow any to become
Judges in his Republic till near to middle life, lest acquaintance with Wrong should harden them into a dis-
trust of Humanity: and acquaintance with Diplomacy is
said to be little less dangerous."

" Though, by-the-way," interposed I, " was not Plato's
Master accused of perplexing those simple Affections
and Impulses of Youth by his Dialectic, and making
premature Sophists of the Etonians of Athens?"

" By Aristophanes, you mean," said Euphranor, with
no mock gravity now; " whose gross caricature help'd
Anytus and Co. to that Accusation which ended in the
murder of the best and wisest Man of all Antiquity."

" Well, perhaps," said I, " he had been sufficiently
punish'd by that termagant Wife of his—whom, by-the-
way, he may have taught to argue with him instead of to
obey. Just as that Son of poor old Strepsiades, in what
you call the Aristophanic Caricature, is taught to rebel
against parental authority, instead of doing as he was
bidden; as he would himself have the Horses to do that
he was spending so much of his Father's money upon:
and as we would have our own Horses, Dogs, and Children,—and young Knights."

" You have got your Heroes into fine company, Euphranor," said Lycion, who, while seeming inattentive to

all that went against him, was quick enough to catch at any turn in his favour.

"Why, let me see," said I, taking up the book again, and|running my eye over the passage—"yes,—*'Ardent* (17) *of desire,'*—*'Tractable,'*—some of them at least—*'Without comprehending much'*—*'Ambitious'*—*'Despisers of Riches'*—*'Warm friends and hearty Companions'*—really very characteristic of the better breed of Dogs and Horses. And why not? The Horse, you know, has given his very name to Chivalry, because of his association in the Heroic Enterprises of Men,—*El mas Hidalgo Bruto,* Calderon calls him. He was sometimes buried, I think, along with our heroic Ancestors—just as some favourite wife was buried along with her husband in the East. So the Muse sings of those who believe their faithful Dog will accompany them to the World of Spirits— as even some wise and good Christian men have thought it not impossible he may, not only because of his Moral, but——"

"Well," said Euphranor, "we need not trouble ourselves about carrying the question quite so far."

"Oh, do not drop your poor kinsman just when you are going into good Company," said Lycion.

"By-the-way, Lycion," said I, "has not your Parliament a 'Whipper-in' of its more dilatory members—or of those often of the younger ones, I think, who may be diverting themselves with some stray scent elsewhere?"

To this he only replied with a long whiff from his Cigar; but Euphranor said:

" Well, come, Lycion, let us take the Doctor at his word, and turn it against himself. For if you and I, in virtue of our Youth, are so inspired with all this Moral that he talks of—why, we—or, rather, you— *are* wanted in Parliament, not only to follow like Dog and Horse, as he pretends, but also to take the lead; so as the (18) |Generous counsel, the νεανικὸν φρόνημα, of Youth, may vivify and ennoble the cold Politic of Age."

" Well, I remember hearing of a young Senator," said I, "who, in my younger days, was celebrated for his faculty of Cock-crowing by way of waking up his more drowsy Seniors, I suppose, about the small hours of the morning—or, perhaps, in token of Victory over an unexpected Minority."

" No, no," said Euphranor, laughing, " I mean seriously; as in the passage we read from Digby, Amyntas, the Man of Policy, was wrong, and his son Alexander right."

But oddly enough, as I remember'd the story in Herodotus, by a device which smack'd more of Policy than Generosity. " But in the other case, Argus, I suppose, was not so wrong in restraining the impetuosity of his Youthful Crew, who,—is it not credibly thought?—would have fail'd, but for Medea's unexpected magical assistance? "

Euphranor was not clear about his.

" Besides," said I, " does not this very νεανικὸν φρόνημα of yours result from that νεανικὸν condition—ἔθος, do you call it?—of Body, in which Youth as assuredly profits as

in the Moral, and which assuredly flows, as from a Fountain of 'Jouvence that rises and runs in the open ' Field
rather than in the Hall of St. Stephen's, where indeed it
is rather likely to get clogg'd, if not altogether dried up?
As, for instance, *Animal Spirit, Animal Courage, Sanguine Temper,* and so forth—all which, by the way, says
Aristotle, inflame Youth not at all like Reasonable people, but ' *like persons drunk with wine* '—all which, for
better or worse, is fermented by Cricket from good Roast
Beef into pure Blood, Muscle—and Moral."

" Chivalry refined into patent Essence of Beef! " said
Euphranor, only half-amused.

" I hope you like the taste of it," said Lycion, under *(19)*
his hat.

" Well, at any rate," said I, laughing, " those young
Argonauts needed a good stock of it to work a much
heavier craft than we have been pulling to-day, when the
wind fail'd them. And yet, with all their animal Inebria-
tion—whencesoever derived—so tractable in their Moral
as to submit at once to their Politic Leader—Argus, was
it not? "

" ' The Nestor of the Party,' Digby calls him," said
Euphranor, " good, old, garrulous Nestor, whom, somehow, I think one seems to feel more at home with than any
of the Homeric Heroes."

" Aye, *he* was entitled to crow in the Grecian Parliament, fine ' Old Cock ' as he was, about the gallant exploits of his Youth, being at threescore so active in Body
as in Spirit, that Agamemnon declares, I think, that Troy

would soon come down had he but a few more such Generals.   Ah yes, Euphranor! could one by so full Apprenticeship of Youth become so thoroughly season'd with its Spirit, that all the Reason of Manhood, and Politic of Age, and Experience of the World, should serve not to freeze, but to direct, the genial Current of the Soul, so that—

'Ev'n while the vital Heat retreats below,
Ev'n while the hoary head is lost in Snow,
The *Life* is in the leaf, and still between
The fits of falling Snow appears the streaky Green'—

that Boy's Heart within the Man's never ceasing to throb and tremble, even to remotest Age—then indeed your Senate would need no other Youth than its Elders to vivify their counsel, or could admit the Young without danger of corrupting them by ignoble Policy.

"Well, come," said Euphranor gaily, after my rather
(20) |sententious peroration, "Lycion need not be condemn'd to enter Parliament—or even ' The World '—unless he pleases, for some twenty years to come, if he will follow Pythagoras, who, you know, Doctor, devotes the first forty years of his Man's allotted Eighty to Childhood and Youth; a dispensation which you and I at least shall not quarrel with."

"No, nor anyone else, I should suppose," said I. " Think, my dear Lycion, what a privilege for you to have yet more than twenty good years' expatiation in the Elysian Cricket-field of Youth before pent up in that

[134   ]

Close Borough of your Father's! And Euphranor, whom we thought fast slipping out of his Prime as his Youth attained a beard, is in fact only just entering upon it. And, most wonderful of all, I, who not only have myself enter'd the World, but made my bread by bringing others into it these fifteen years, have myself only just ceased to be a Boy!"

What reply Lycion might have deign'd to all this, I know not; for just now one of his friends looked out again from the Billiard-room window, and called out to him, "the coast was clear." On which Lycion getting up, and muttering something about its being a pity we did not go back to Trap-ball, and I retorting that we could carry it forward into Life with us, he carelessly nodded to us both, and with an *"Au Revoir"* lounged with his Cigar into the house.

Then Euphranor and I took each a draught of the good liquor which Lycion had declined to share with us; and, on setting down his tumbler, he said:

"Ah! you should have heard our friend Skythrops commenting on that Inventory of Youth, as you call it, which he happen'd to open upon in my rooms the other day."

"Perhaps the book is rather apt to open there of its own accord," said I. "Well—and what did old Skythrops say?" *(21)*

"Oh, you may anticipate — 'the same old Heathen talk,' he said—' very well for a Pagan to write, and a Papist to quote—' and, according to you, Doctor, for

Horse and Dog to participate in, and for Bullock to supply."

"But I had been mainly bantering Lycion," I said; "as Euphranor also, I supposed with his Pythagorean disposition of Life. Lycion would not much have cared had I derived them from the angels. As for that Animal condition to which I had partly referr'd them, we Doctors were of old notorious on that score, not choosing your Moralist and Philosopher to carry off all the fee. But 'The Cobbler to his Last'—or, the Tailor to his Goose, if I might be call'd in, as only I profess'd, to accommodate the outer Man with what Sterne calls his Jerkin, leaving its Lining to your Philosopher and Divine."

"Sterne!" ejaculated Euphranor; "just like him— Soul and Body all of a piece."

"Nay, nay," said I, laughing; "your Lining is often of a finer material, you know."

"And often of a coarser, as in Sterne's own case, I believe."

"Well, then, I would turn Mason, or Bricklayer," I said; "and confine myself to the House of Clay, in which, as the Poets tell us, the Soul is Tenant—'The Body's Guest'—as Sir Walter Raleigh calls him; would that do?"

".Better, at any rate, than Jerkin and Lining."

But here the same difficulty presented itself. For, however essentially distinct the Tenant from his Lodging, his Health, as we of the material Faculty believed, in some

|measure depended on the salubrity of the House, in *(22)* which he is not merely a Guest, but a Prisoner, and from which I knew Euphranor thought he was forbidden to escape by any violent self-extrication. Dryden indeed tells us of—

"A fiery Soul that, working out its way,
Fretted the pigmy Body to decay,
And o'er-informed this Tenement of Clay."—

" But *that* was the Soul of an Achitophel," Euphranor argued, " whose collapse, whether beginning from within or without, was of less than little moment to the world. But the truly grand Soul possesses himself in peace, or, if he suffer from self-neglect, or over-exertion in striving after the good of others—why, that same Dryden—or Waller, it may be—says that such an one becomes, not weaker, but stronger, by that Bodily decay, whether of Infirmity, or of Old Age, which lets in new light through the chinks of dilapidation—if not, as my loftier Words-worth has it, some rays of that Original Glory which he brought with him to be darken'd in the Body at Birth."

" But then," I said, " if your crazy Cottage won't fall to pieces at once, but, after the manner of creaking gates, go creaking—or, as the Sailors say of their boats, ' com-plaining ' on—making the Tenant, and most likely all his Neighbours, complain also, and perpetually calling on the Tenant for repairs, and this when he wants to be about other more important Business of his own? To think how much time—and patience—a Divine Soul has to

[137]

waste over some little bit of Cheese, perhaps, that, owing to bad drainage, will stick in the stomach of an otherwise Seraphic Doctor."

Euphranor laughed a little; and I went on; " Better
(23) |surely, for all sakes, to build up for her—as far as we may—for we cannot yet ensure the foundation—a spacious, airy, and wholesome Tenement becoming so Divine a Tenant, of so strong a foundation and masonry as to resist the wear and tear of Elements without, and herself within. Yes; and a *handsome* house withal—unless indeed you think the handsome Soul will fashion that about herself from within—like a shell—which, so far as her Top-storey, where she is supposed chiefly to reside, I think may be the case."

" Ah," said Euphranor, " one of the most beautiful of all human Souls, as I think, could scarce accomplish that."

" Socrates? " said I. " No; but did not he profess that his Soul was naturally an ugly soul to begin with? So, by the time he had beautified her within, it was too late to re-front her Outside, which had case-hardened, I suppose. But did not he accompany Alcibiades, not only because of his Spiritual, but also of his Physical Beauty, in which, as in the Phidian statues, the Divine Original of Man was supposed to reflect Himself, and which has been accepted as such by Christian Art, and indeed by all Peoples who are furthest removed from that of the Beast? "

" Even of Dog and Horse? " said Euphranor, smiling.

" Even my sturdy old Philosopher Montaigne—who,

by the way, declares that he rates 'La Beauté à deux doigts de la Bonté . . . non seulement aux hommes qui me servent, mais aux bêtes aussi'—quotes your Aristotle, saying that we owe a sort of Homage to those who resemble the Statues of the Gods as to the Statues themselves. And thus Socrates may have felt about Alcibiades, who, in those earlier and better days when Socrates knew him, might almost be taken as a counterpart of the Picture of Youth, with all its Virtues and defects, which Aristotle has drawn for us."

" Or, what do you say, Doctor, to Aristotle's own Pupil, *(24)* Alexander, who turned out a yet more astonishing Phenomenon?—I wonder, Doctor, what you, with all your theories, would have done had such an ' Enfant terrible ' as either of them been put into your hands."

" Well, at any rate, I should have the advantage of first laying hold of him on coming into the World, which was not the case with Aristotle, or with the Doctors of his time, was it? "

Euphranor thought not.

" However, I know not yet whether I have ever had an Infant Hero of any kind to deal with; none, certainly, who gave any indication of any such ' clouds of glory ' as your Wordsworth tells of, even when just arrived from their several homes—in Alexander's case, of a somewhat sulphureous nature, according to Skythrops, I doubt. No, nor of any young Wordsworth neither under our diviner auspices."

" Nay, but," said Euphranor, " he tells us that our

Birth is but a ' Sleep and a forgetting ' of something
which must take some waking-time to develope."

" But which, if I remember aright, is to begin to darken
' with shades of the Prison-house,' as Wordsworth calls it,
that begin to close about ' the growing Boy.' But I am
too much of a Philistine, as you Germans have it, to comprehend the Transcendental. All I know is, that I have
not yet detected any signs of the ' Heaven that lies about
our Infancy,' nor for some while after—no, not even
peeping through those windows through which the Soul
is said more immediately to look, but as yet with no more
speculation in them than those of the poor whelp of the
Dog we talked of—in spite of a nine days' start of him."

(25)   " Nevertheless," said Euphranor, " I have heard tell of
another Poet's saying that he knew of no human outlook
so solemn as that from an Infant's Eyes; and how it was
from those of his own he learn'd that those of the Divine
Child in Raffaelle's Sistine Madonna were not over-
charged with expression, as he had previously thought
they might be."

" I think," said I, " you must have heard of that from
me, who certainly did hear something like it from the
Poet himself, who used to let fall—not lay down—the
word that settled the question, æsthetic or other, which
others hammer'd after in vain. Yes; that was on occasion, I think, of his having watch'd his Child one morning
' worshipping the Sunbeam on the Bed-post '—I suppose
the worship of Wonder, such as I have heard grown-up
Children tell of at first sight of the Alps, or Niagara;

or such stay-at-home Islanders as ourselves at first sight of the Sea, from such a height as Flamborough Head."

" Some farther-seeing Wonder than dog or kitten are conscious of, at any rate," said Euphranor.

" Ah, who knows? I have seen both of them watching that very Sunbeam too—the Kitten perhaps playing with it, to be sure. If but the Philosopher or Poet could live in the Child's or kitten's Brain for a while! The Bed-post Sun-worship, however, was of a Child of several months—and Raffaelle's—a full year old, would you say?"

" Nay, you know about such matters better than I," said Euphranor, laughing.

" Well, however it may be with young Wordsworth, Raffaelle's child certainly *was* ' drawing Clouds of Glory ' from *His* Home, and we may suppose him conscious of it —|yes, and of his Mission to dispense that glory to the (26) World. And I remember how the same Poet also noticed the Attitude of the Child, which might otherwise seem somewhat too magisterial for his age."

Euphranor knew the Picture by Engraving only; but he observed how the Divine Mother's eyes also were dilated, not as with Human Mother's Love, but as with awe and Wonder at the Infant she was presenting to the World, as if silently saying, " Behold your King! "

" Why," said I, " do not some of you believe the ' Clouds of Glory ' to have been drawn directly from herself? "

[141]

" Nonsense, nonsense, Doctor—you know better, as did Raffaelle also, I believe, in spite of the Pope."

" Well, well," said I, " your Wordsworth Boy has also his Divine Mission to fulfil in confessing that of Raffaelle's. But, however it may be with that Mother and Child, does not one—of your Germans, I think—say that, with us mortals, it is from the Mother's eyes that Religion dawns into the Child's Soul?—the Religion of Love, at first, I suppose, in gratitude for the flowing breast and feeding hand below."

" Perhaps—in some degree," said Euphranor. " As you were saying of that Sun-worshipper, one cannot fathom how far the Child may see into the Mother's eyes any more than all that is to be read in them."

" To be developed between them thereafter, I suppose," said I, " when the Mother's lips interpret the Revelation of her Eyes, and lead up from her Love to the perception of some Invisible Parent of all."

" Ah," said Euphranor, " how well I remember learning to repeat after her, every morning and night, ' Our Father which art in Heaven.' "

(27) " In your little white Surplice, like Sir Joshua's little Samuel—on whom the Light is dawning direct from Heaven, I think—from Him to whom you were half-articulately praying to ' make me a dood Boy ' to them. And, by-and-by, Watts and Jane Taylor's, of the Star Daisy in the grass, and the Stars in Heaven.

'For ever singing as they shine,
The Hand that made us is Divine.' "

[142]

" Ah," said Euphranor, " and beautiful some of those early things of Watts and Jane Taylor are. They run in my head still."

" As why should they not? " said I, " you being yet in your Childhood, you know. Why, I, who have left it some way behind me, to be sure, am constantly reminded of them in the nurseries I am so often call'd into from which they are not yet banisht by more æsthetic verse. As also, I must say, of some yet more early, and profane, such as ' Rock-a-bye Baby on the Tree-top,' with that catastrophe which never fail'd to ' bring the House down ' along with the Bough which is,—Mother's Arms. Then there was ' Little Bopeep whose stray flock came back to her of themselves, carrying their tails behind them '—and ' Little Boy Blue ' who was less fortunate. Ah, what a pretty little picture he makes ' under the haycock '— like one of your Greek Idylls, I think, and quite ' suitable to this present Month of May,' as old Izaak says. Let me hear if you remember it, Sir."

And Euphranor, like a good boy, repeated the verses.*

" And then," said I, " the echoes of those old London (28) Bells whose Ancestors once recall'd Whittington back to be their Lord Mayor: and now communicating from their several Steeples as to how the account with St. Clement's was to be paid—which, by-the-by, I remember

---

* " *Little Boy Blue, come blow your horn;*
The Cow's in the meadow, the Sheep in the corn.
Is this the way you mind your Sheep,
Under the haycock fast asleep ? "

"*The* 'meadow,' " *said I, by way of annotation, "being, you know, of grass reserved for meadowing, or mowing.*"

[143]

being thus summarily settled by an old College Friend
of mine—

'Confound you all!
Said the Great Bell of Paul';

only, I am afraid, with something more Athanasian than
'Confound '—though he was not then a Dignitary of the
Church.   Then that Tragedy of 'Cock Robin '—the Fly
that saw it with that little Eye of his—and the Owl with
his spade and *'Showl'*—proper old word that too—and
the Bull who the Bell could pull — and — but I doubt
whether you will approve of the Rook reading the Burial
Service, nor do I like bringing the Lark, only for a
rhyme's sake, down from Heaven, to make the responses.
And all this illustrated by appropriate ' Gays,'—as they
call them in Suffolk—and recited, if not intoned, according to the different Characters."

" Plato's ' Music of Education,' I suppose," said Euphranor.

" Yes," said I, warming with my subject; " and then,
beside the True Histories of Dog and Horse whose
example is to be followed, Fables that treat of others,
Lions, Eagles, Asses, Foxes, Cocks, and other feather'd
or four-footed Creatures, who, as in Cock Robin's case,
(29) |talk as well as act, but with a Moral—more or less com-
mendable—provided *the* Moral be dropt.   Then as your
punning friend Plato, you told me, says that *Thaumas*—
Wonder—is Father of Iris, who directly communicates
between Heaven and Earth—as in the case of that Bed-

post-kissing Apollo—you, being a pious man, doubtless
had your Giants, Genii, Enchanters, Fairies, Ogres,
Witches, Ghosts——"

But Euphranor was decidedly against admitting any
Ghost into the Nursery, and even Witches, remembering
little Lamb's childish terror at Her of Endor.

"Oh, but," said I, "*She* was a real Witch, you know,
though represented by Stackhouse; who need not figure
among the Musicians, to be sure. You, however, as Lycion says, have your Giants and Dragons to play with—by
way of Symbol, if you please—and you must not grudge
your younger Brethren in Arms that redoubtable JACK
who slew the Giants whom you are to slay over again, and
who for that very purpose climb'd up a Bean-stalk some
way at least to Heaven—an Allegory that, as Sir Thomas
Browne says, 'admits of a wide solution.'"

"Ah," said my companion, "I remember how you used
to climb up the Poplar in our garden by way of Bean-
stalk, looking out upon us now and then, till lost among
the branches. You could not do that now, Doctor."

"No more than I could up Jack's own Bean-stalk. I
was a thin slip of a Knight then, not long turned of
Twenty, I suppose—almost more like a Giant than a
Jack to the rest of you—but children do not mind such
disproportions. No—I could better play one of the three
Bears growling for his mess of porridge now. But, in
default of my transcendental illustration of Jack, he and
his like are well represented in such Effigies as your friend (30)
Plato never dream'd of in his philosophy, though Phidias

and Praxiteles may have sketcht for their Children what
now is multiplied by Engraving into every Nursery."

"Not to mention Printing, to read about what is represented," said Euphranor.

"I do not know what to say about *that*," said I. "Does
not your Philosopher repudiate any but Oral instruction?"

"Notwithstanding all which, I am afraid we must learn
to read," said Euphranor, "in these degenerate days."

"Well, if needs must," said I, "you may learn in the
most musical way of all. Do you not remember the practice of our Forefathers?

'To Master John, the Chamber-maid
A Horn-book gives of Ginger-bread;
And, that the Child may learn the better,
As he can name, he eats the Letter.'

"Oh, how I used to wish," said Euphranor, "there had
been any such royal road to Grammar which one had to
stumble over some years after."

" Well," said I, " but there is now, I believe, a Comic
Grammar—as well as a Comic History of Rome—and of
England."

"Say no more of all that, pray, Doctor. The old 'Propria quæ maribus' was better Music, uncouth as it was, and
almost as puzzling as an Oracle. I am sure it is only now
—when I try—that I understand the meaning of the rule
I then repeated mechanically—like a Parrot you would
say."

"Sufficiently intelligible, however," said I, "to be

mechanically applied in distinguishing the different parts
|of Speech, and how related to one another; how a verb *(31)*
governs an accusative, and an adjective agrees with a
noun; to all which you are guided by certain terminations
of *us, a, um,* and *do, das, dat,* and so on; till you are
able to put the scattered words together, and so ford
through a sentence. And the old uncouth Music, as you
call it, nevertheless served to fix those rules in the
memory."

"But all that is changed now!" said Euphranor;
" Nominative and Accusative are turned into Subjective,
Objective, and what not."

" Darkening the unintelligible to Boys," said I, " whatever it may afterwards to men. ' Floreat Etona!' say I,
with her old Lily, and ' Propria quæ maribus,' always pro-
viding there be not too much of it—even could it be con-
strued, like the Alphabet, into Ginger-bread."

" Well," said Euphranor, " I think you took pretty
good care that we should not suffer an indigestion of the
latter, when you were among us at home, Doctor. What
with mounting that Bean-stalk yourself, and clearing us
out of the Schoolroom into the Garden, wet or dry, re-
gardless of Aunt's screaming from the window for us to
come in, when a Cloud was coming up in the Sky——"

" Or a little dew lying on the Grass."

" Why, I believe you would have a Child's shoes made
with holes in them on purpose to let in water, as Locke
recommends," said Euphranor, laughing.

" I wouldn't keep him within for having none, whole

[147]

shoes, or whole clothes—no, nor *any*—only the Police would interfere."

" But the Child catches cold."

" Put him to bed and dose him."

" But he dies."

(32)   " Then, as a sensible woman said, ' is provided for.' Your own Plato, I think, says it is better the weakly ones should die at once; and the Spartans, I think, kill'd them off."

" Come, come, Doctor," said Euphranor. " I really think you gave us colds on purpose to be called in to cure them."

" No, no; that was before I was a Doctor, you know. But I doubt that I was the Lord of Mis-rule sometimes, though, by the way, I am certain that I sometimes recommended a remedy, not when you were sick, but when you were sorry—without a cause—I mean, obstinate, or self-willed against the little Discipline you had to submit to."

Euphranor looked comically at me.

" Yes," said I, " you know—a slap on that part where the Rod is to be applied in after years—and which I had, not long before, suffered myself."

" *That* is almost out of date now, along with other Spartan severities even in Criminal cases," said Euphranor.

" Yes, and the more the pity in both cases. How much better in the Child's than being shut up, or additionally tasked—revenging a temporary wrong with a lasting injury. And, as for your public Criminal—my wonder is that even modern squeamishness does not see that a public application of the Rod or Lash on the bare back in the Marketplace would be more likely to daunt the Culprit, and all Beholders, from future Misdemeanour than months of imprisonment, well-boarded, lodged, and cared for, at the Country's cost."

" Nevertheless," said Euphranor, " I do not remember your Advice being taken in our case, much as I, for one, may have deserved it."

" No," said I; " your Father was gone, you know, and (33) your Mother too tender-hearted — indulgent, I might say."

" Which, with all your Spartan discipline, I know you think the better extreme," said Euphranor.

" Oh, far the better!" said I—" letting the *Truth* come to the surface—the ugliest Truth better than the fairest Falsehood which Fear naturally brings with it, and all the better for determining outwardly, as we Doctors say, than repressed to rankle within. Why, even without fear of spank or Rod, you remember how your Wordsworth's little Harry was taught the practice of Lying, who, simply being teased with well-meaning questions as to *why* he liked one place better than another, caught at a Weather-cock for a reason *why*. Your mother was wiser than that. I dare say she did not bother you about the meaning of the Catechism she taught you, provided you generally understood that you were to keep your hands from picking and stealing, and your tongue from evil-speaking, lying, and slandering. She did not insist, as Skythrops would

[149]

have had you, on your owning yourselves Children of
the Devil."

" No, no! "

" I should not even wonder if, staunch Churchwoman
as she was, she did not condemn you to go more than once
of a Sunday to Church—perhaps not to be shut up for
two hours' morning Service in a Pew, without being al-
lowed to go to sleep there; nor tease you about Text and
Sermon afterward. For, if she had, you would not, I
believe, have been the determined Churchman you are."

" Ah, I remember so well," said Euphranor, " her tell-
(34) ing|a stricter neighbour of ours that, for all she saw, the
Child generally grew up with clean opposite inclinations
and ways of thinking, from the Parent."

" Yes," said I, " that is the way from Parent to Child,
and from Generation to Generation; and so the World
goes round."

" And we—Brothers and Sister, I mean "— said Euphranor, " now catch ourselves constantly saying how
right she was in the few things we ever thought her mistaken about. God bless her! "

He took a long pull at his glass, and was silent some
little while—she had died a few years ago—and then he
said:

" However, even she began in time to find ' the Boys
too much for her,' as she said—for which you, Doctor, as
you say, are partly accountable; besides, we should have
our livelihood to earn, unlike your born Heroes; and
must begin to work sooner rather than later. Our Friend

[150]

Skythrops' *ipse* had already warned her of our innate, and steadily growing, Depravity, and, when I was seven or eight years old, came to propose taking me under his wing, at what he called his ' Seminary for young Gentlemen.' "

" I see him," said I, " coming up the shrubbery walk in a white tie, and with a face of determined asperity— the edge of the Axe now turned *toward* the Criminal. Aye, I was gone away to Edinburgh by that time; indeed I think he waited till I was well out of the way. Well, what did he say? "

" Oh, he explained his scheme, whatever it was——"

" And—oh, I can tell you—some eight or ten hours a day of Grammar and Arithmetic, Globes, History, and as Dickens says, 'General Christianity'; and, by way of *(35)* Recreation, two hours' daily walk with himself and his sallow Pupils, two and two along the Highroad, improved with a running commentary by Skythrops—with perhaps a little gymnastic gallows in his gravel Play-ground, without room or time for any generous exercise. Your mother, I hope, gave him a biscuit and a glass of Sherry, and, with all due thanks, let him go back the way he came."

" His Plan does not please you, Doctor? "

" And if it did—and it only wanted reversing—*he* would not. No Boy with any Blood in his veins can profit from a Teacher trying to graft from dead wood upon the living sapling. Even the poor Women's '*Preparatory Establishments*' for ' Young Gentlemen ' are better; however narrow their notions and routine, they

[151]

do not at heart dislike a little of the Devil in the other sex, however intolerant of him in their own."

" Well, we were committed to neither," said Euphranor, " but to a nice young Fellow who came to be Curate in the Parish, and who taught us at home, little but well —among other things—a little Cricket."

" Bravo! " said I.

" Then Uncle James, you know, hearing that I was rather of a studious turn—' serious,' he called it—took it into his head that one of his Brother's family should be a Parson, and so undertook to pay my way at Westminster, which he thought an aristocratic School, and handy for him in the City. In which, perhaps, you do not disagree with him, Doctor? "

" No," said I; " though not bred up at any of them myself, I must confess I love the great ancient, Royal, aye, and aristocratic Foundations—Eton with her ' Henry's
(36) |holy Shade '—why, Gray's verses were enough to endear it to me—and under the walls of his Royal Castle, all reflected in the water of old Father Thames, as he glides down the valley; and Winchester with her William of Wykeham entomb'd in the Cathedral he built beside his School——"

" And *West*minster, if you please, Doctor, under the Shadow of its glorious old Abbey, where Kings are crown'd and buried, and with Eton's own River flowing beside it in ampler proportions."

" Though not so sweet," said I. " However, excepting that fouler water—and fouler air—and some other less wholesome associations inseparable from such a City, I am quite ready to pray for your Westminster among those other 'Royal and Religious Foundations' whom the Preacher invites us to pray for at St. Mary's. But with Eton we began, you know, looking with Charles Lamb and his Friend at the fine Lads there playing; and there I will leave them to enjoy it while they may, 'strangers yet to Pain'—and Parliament—to sublime their Beef-steak into Chivalry in that famous Cricket-field of theirs by the side of old Father Thames murmuring of so many Generations of chivalric Ancestors."

"We must call down Lycion to return thanks for *that* compliment," said Euphranor; "he is an Eton man, as were his Fathers before him, you know, and, I think, proud, as your Etonians are, of his School, in spite of his affected Indifference."

"Do you know what sort of a Lad he was while there?" said I.

"Oh, always the Gentleman."

"Perhaps somewhat too much so for a Boy."

"No, no, I do no mean that—I mean essentially honour-|able, truthful, and not deficient in courage, I believe, *(37)* whenever it was called for; but indolent, and perhaps fonder too of the last new Novel, and the Cigar and Easy-chair, to exert himself in the way you like."

"Preparing for the Club, Opera, Opera-glass, '*Déjeuner dansant,*' etcetera, if not for active service in Parliament. Eton should provide for those indolent Children of hers."

[153]

" Well, she has provided her field, and old Father
Thames, as you say, and Boys are supposed to take pretty
good care of themselves in making use of them."

" Not always, however, as we see in Lycion's case, nor
of others, who, if they do not ' sacrifice the Living Man
to the Dead Languages,' dissipate him among the Fine
Arts, Music, Poetry, Painting, and the like, in the inter-
val. Why, did not those very Greeks of whom you make
so much—and, as I believe, your modern Germans—make
Gymnastic a necessary part of their education? "

" But you would not have Eton Boys compelled to
climb and tumble like monkeys over gymnastic poles and
gallows as we saw with Skythrops' ' Young Gentlemen '? "

" Perhaps not; but what do you say now to some good
Military Drill, with March, Counter-march, Encounter,
Bivouac ' Wacht am Rhein '—Encampment—that is, by
Father Thames—and such-like Exercises for which Eton
has ample room, and which no less a Man—although a
Poet—than John Milton, enjoin'd as the proper preparation for War, and, *I* say, carrying along with them a sense
of Order, Self-restraint, and Mutual Dependence, no less
necessary in all the relations of Peace? "

" We might all of us have been the better for that, I
suppose," said Euphranor.

(38) " And only think," said I, "if—as in some German
School — Fellenberg's, I think — there were, beside the
Playground, a piece of Arable to *work in*—perhaps at
a daily wage of provender according to the work done—

what illumination might some young Lycion receive, as
to the condition of the Poor, ' unquenchable by logic and
statistics,' says Carlyle, ' when he comes, as Duke of
Logwood, to legislate in Parliament.' "

" Better Log than Brute, however," answer'd Euphranor. " You must beware, Doctor, lest with all your
Ploughing and other Beef-compelling Accomplishments
you do not sink the Man in the Animal, as was much the
case with our ' Hereditary Rulers ' of some hundred years
ago."

" 'Μηδὲν ἄγαν,' " said I; "let us but lay in—when only
laid in it can be—such a store of that same well-concocted
stuff as shall last us all Life's journey through, with all
its ups and downs.   Nothing, say the Hunters, that Blood
and Bone won't get over."

" Be there a good Rider to guide him! " said Euphranor; " and *that,* in Man's case, I take it is—if not yet
the Reason we talked of—a Moral such as no Beast that
breathes is conscious of.   You talk of this Animal virtue,
and that—why, for instance, is there not a *moral,* as dis-
tinguisht from an *animal* Courage, to face, not only the
sudden danger of the field, but something far-off coming, far foreseen, and far more terrible—Cranmer's for
instance——"

" Which," said I, " had all but failed—all the more
honour for triumphing at last!   But Hugh Latimer,
I think, had wrought along with his Father's hinds in
Leicestershire.   Anyhow, there is no harm in having two
strings to your Bow, whichever of them be the strongest. *(39)*

[155   ]

The immortal Soul obliged, as she is, to take the Field
of Mortality, would not be the worse for being mounted
on a good Animal, though I must not say with the Hunters, till the Rider seems ' part of his horse.' As to your
Reason—he is apt to *crane* a little too much over the '
hedge, as they say, till, by too long considering the
'*How,*' he comes to question the '*Why,*' and, the longer
looking, the less liking, shirks it altogether, or by his
Indecision brings Horse and Rider into the Ditch. Hamlet lets us into the secret—luckily for us enacting the very
moral he descants on—when he reflects on his own imbe-
cility of action:

> " ' Whether it be
> Bestial oblivion, or some craven scruple
> Of thinking too precisely on the Event,
> A thought which, quarter'd, hath but one part Wisdom,
> And ever three parts Coward—I do not know
> Why yet I live to say, "*This thing's to do,*"
> Sith I have Cause, and Will, and Strength, and Means,
> To do't.'

Not in his case surely '*oblivion,*' with such reminders,
supernatural and other, as he had: nor as in our case,
with the Ditch before our Eyes: nor want of Courage,
which was his Royal inheritance; but the *Will,* which he
reckon'd on as surely as on Strength and Means—was
he so sure of *that?* He had previously told us how ' The
native hue of Resolution '—how like that glow upon the
cheek of healthy Youth!—

' The native hue of Resolution,
Is sickled o'er with the pale cast of Thought,
And Enterprises of great pith and moment
With this regard, their currents turn awry,
And lose the name of Action.'

He had, he tells his College Friends, forgone his '*Cus-* (40)
tom of Exercises '—among others, perhaps, his Cricket,
at Wittenberg too soon, and taken to reasoning about ' To
be, or not to be '—otherwise he would surely have bowl'd
his wicked uncle down at once."

  " Though not without calling ' Play! ' I hope," said
Euphranor, laughing.

  " At any rate, not while his Adversary's back was
turned, and so far prepared, inasmuch as he was engaged
in repentant Prayer.   And that is the reason Hamlet
gives for not then despatching him, lest, being so employ'd, he should escape the future punishment of his
crime.   An odd motive for the youthful Moral to have
reasoned itself into."

  " His Father had been cut off unprepared, and perhaps, according to the Moral of those days, could only
be avenged by such a plenary Expiation."

  " Perhaps; or, perhaps—and Shakespeare himself may
not have known exactly why—Hamlet only made it an
excuse for delaying what he had to do, as delay he does,
till vengeance seems beyond his reach when he suffers
himself to be sent out of the country.   For you know
the *Habit* of Resolving without Doing, as in the Closet,

[157   ]

gradually snaps the connexion between them, and the case becomes chronically hopeless."

Euphranor said that I had stolen that fine Moral of mine from a Volume of " Newman's Sermons " which he had lent me, as I agreed with him was probably the case; and then he said:

" Well, Bowling down a King is, I suppose, a ticklish Business, and the Bowler may miss his aim by being too long about taking it: but, in Cricket proper, I have most *(41)* wonder'd at the Batter who has to decide|whether to block, strike, or tip, in that twinkling of an eye between the ball's delivery, and its arrival at his wicket."

" Yes," said I, " and the Boxer who puts in a blow with one hand at the same moment of warding one off with the other."

" ' Gladiatorem in arenâ,' " said Euphranor.

" Yes; what is called *'Presence of mind,'* where there is not time to *'make it up.'* And all the more necessary and remarkable in proportion to the Danger involved. As when the Hunter's horse falling with him in full cry, he braces himself, between saddle and ground, to pitch clear of his horse—as Fielding tells us that brave old Parson Adams did, when probably thinking less of his horse than of those Sermons he carried in his saddle-bags."

" Ah! " said Euphranor, " Parson Adams was so far a lucky man to have a Horse at all, which we poor fellows now can hardly afford. I remember how I used to envy those who—for the fun, if for nothing else—followed brave old Sedgwick across country, thorough brier, thorough mire.   Ah! *that* was a Lecture after your own heart, Doctor; something more than peripatetic, and from one with plenty of the Boy in him when over Seventy, I believe."

" Well, there again," said I, " your great Schools might condescend to take another hint from abroad where some one—Fellenberg again, I think—had a Riding-house in his much poorer School, where you might learn not only to sit your horse if ever able to provide one for yourself, but also to saddle, bridle, rub him down, with the 's'ss-s'ss' which I fancy was heard on the morning of Agincourt—if, by the way, one horse was left in all the host."

" Well, come," said Euphranor, " the Gladiator, at any |rate, is gone—and the Boxer after him—and the Hunter, *(42)* I think, going after both; perhaps the very Horse he rides gradually to be put away by Steam into some Museum among the extinct Species that Man has no longer room or business for."

" Nevertheless," said I.   " War is *not* gone with the Gladiator, and cannon and rifle yet leave room for hand-to-hand conflict, as may one day—which God forbid!—come to proof in our own sea-girt Island.   If safe from abroad, some Ruffian may still assault you in some shady lane—nay, in your own parlour—at home, when you have nothing but your own strong arm, and ready soul to direct it.   Accidents will happen in the best-regulated families. The House will take fire, the Coach will break down, the Boat will upset;—is there no gentleman who can swim, to save himself and others; no one do more to save the Maid

snoring in the garret, than helplessly looking on—or turning away? Some one is taken ill at midnight; John is
drunk in bed; is there no Gentleman can saddle Dobbin
—much less get a Collar over his Head, or the Crupper
over his tail, without such awkwardness as brings on his
abdomen the kick he fears, and spoils him for the journey?
And I do maintain," I continued, " having now gotten
' the bit between my teeth'—maintain against all Comers
that, independent of any bodily action on their part, these,
and the like Accomplishments, as you call them, do carry
with them, and, I will say, with the Soul incorporate, that
habitual Instinct of Courage, Resolution, and Decision,
which, together with the Good Humour which good
animal Condition goes so far to ensure, do, I say, prepare
and arm the Man not only against the greater, but against
those minor Trials of Life which are so far harder to
(43) encounter|because of perpetually cropping up; and thus
do cause him to radiate, if through a narrow circle, yet,
through that, imperceptibly to the whole world, a happier
atmosphere about him than could be inspired by Closet-
loads of Poetry, Metaphysic, and Divinity. No doubt
there is danger, as you say, of the Animal overpowering
the Rational, as, I maintain, equally so of the reverse;
no doubt the high-mettled Colt will be likeliest to run
riot, as may my Lad, inflamed with Aristotle's ' Wine of
Youth,' into excesses which even the virtuous Berkeley
says are the more curable as lying in the Passions;
whereas, says he, ' the dry Rogue who sets up for Judgment is incorrigible.' But, whatever be the result, VIGOUR,

[160]

of Body, as of Spirit, one must have, subject like all good
things to the worst corruption—Strength itself, even of
Evil, being a kind of *Virtus* which Time, if not good
Counsel, is pretty sure to moderate; whereas Weakness
is the one radical and Incurable Evil, increasing with
every year of Life.—Which fine Moral, or to that effect,
you will also find somewhere in those Sermons, whose
Authority I know you cannot doubt."

"And thus," said Euphranor, "after this long tirade,
you turn out the young Knight from Cricket on the
World."

"Nay," said I, "did I not tell you from the first I
would not meddle with your Digby any more than your
Wordsworth? I have only been talking of ordinary mankind so as to provide for Locke's *'totus, teres,'* and—except in the matter of waistband—'*rotundus*' man, sufficiently accoutred for the campaign of ordinary Life. And
yet, on second thought, I do not see why he should not
do very fairly well for one of the ' Table-round,' if King
|Arthur himself is to be looked for, and found, as the Poet ⟨44⟩
says, in the ' Modern Gentleman,' whose ' stateliest port '
will not be due to the Reading-desk, or Easy-chair. At
any rate, he will be sufficiently qualified, not only to shoot
the Pheasant and hunt the Fox, but even to sit on the
Bench of Magistrates—or even of Parliament—not un-
provided with a quotation or two from Horace or Virgil."

Euphranor could not deny that, laughing.

"Or if obliged, poor fellow—Younger son, perhaps—
to *do* something to earn him Bread—or Claret—for his

Old Age, if not prematurely knocked on the head—
whether not well-qualified for Soldier or Sailor? "

" Nor that."

" As for the Church, (which is your other Gentlemanly
Profession,) you know your Bishop can consecrate Tom
or Blifil equally by that Imposition——"

" Doctor, Doctor," broke in Euphranor, " you have
been talking very well; don't spoil it by one of your
grimaces."

" Well, well," said I,—"Oh, but there is still THE LAW,
in which I would rather trust myself with Tom than
Blifil," added I. " Well, what else? Surgery? which is
said to need ' the Lion's Heart.' "

" But also the Lady's Hand," replied he, smiling.

" Not in drawing one of the Molares, I assure you.
However, thus far I do not seem to have indisposed him
for the Professions which his Rank usually opens to him;
or perhaps even, if he had what you call a Genius in any
direction, might, amid all his Beef-compelling Exercises,
light upon something, as Pan a-hunting, and, as it were
(45) ' unaware,' says Bacon, discover'd that Ceres whom|
the more seriously-searching Gods had looked for in
vain."

" Not for the sake of *Rent*, I hope," said Euphranor,
laughing.

" Or even a turn for looking into Digby and Aristotle,
as into a Mirror—could he but distinguish his own face
in it."

Euphranor, upon whose face no sign of any such self-consciousness appeared, sat for a little while silent, and then said:

"Do you remember that fine passage in Aristophanes' Clouds—lying libel as it is—between the Δίκαιος and Ἄδικος Λόγος?"

I had forgotten, I said, my little Latin and less Greek; and he declared I must however read this scene over again with him. "It is, you see, Old Athens pleading against Young; whom after denouncing, for relinquishing the hardy Discipline and simple severe Exercises that reared the Μαραθωνομάχους Ἄνδρας for the Warm Bath, the Dance, and the Law Court; he suddenly turns to the Young Man who stands hesitating between them, and in those Verses, musical—

ἈΛΛ᾽ οὖν λιπαρός γε καὶ εὐανθής—"

"Come, my good fellow," said I, "you must interpret." And Euphranor, looking down, in undertone repeated:

"O listen to me, and so shall you be stout-hearted and fresh as a
    Daisy;
Not ready to chatter on every matter, nor bent over books till
    you're hazy:
No splitter of straws, no dab at the Laws, making black seem
    white so cunning;
But scamp'ring down out o' the town, and over the green Meadow
    running.
Race, wrestle, and play with your fellows so gay, like so many *(46)*
    Birds of a feather,

[163]

All breathing of Youth, Good-humour, and Truth, in the time of
   the jolly Spring weather,
In the jolly Spring-time, when the Poplar and Lime dishevel their
   tresses together."

"Well, but go on," said I, when he stopp'd, "I am
sure there is something more of it, now you recall the
passage to me—about broad shoulders and——"
   But this was all he had cared to remember.
   I then asked him who was the translator; to which he
replied with a shy smile, 'twas more a paraphrase than a
translation, and I might criticise it as I liked. To which
I had not much to object, I said—perhaps the trees " di-
shevelling their tresses " a little Cockney; which he agreed
it was.* And then, turning off, observed how the degra-
dation which Aristophanes satirized in the Athenian youth
went on and on, so that, when Rome came to help Greece
against Philip of Macedon, the Athenians, says Livy,
could contribute little to the common cause but declama-
tion and despatches—' quibus solum valent.'
   "Aye," said I, " and to think that when Livy was so
writing of Athens, his own Rome was just beginning to
go downhill in the same way and for the same causes:

'Nescit equo rudis

Hærere ingenuus puer,

Venarique timet, ludere doctior

* On a subsequent reference to the original, We expanded the last
line into the following Couplet—whether for better or worse:
   Until with a cool reed drawn from the pool of a neighbouring Water-
      nymph crown'd, you
   Lie stretcht at your ease in the shade of the trees that whisper above
      and around you. [Note added in final addition.]

Græco seu jubeas trocho,
Seu malis vetitâ legibus aleâ:' *

unlike those early times, when Heroic Father begot
and bred Heroic Son; Generation following Generation,
crown'd with Laurel and with Oak; under a system of
|Education, the same Livy says, handed down, as it were *(47)*
an Art, from the very foundation of Rome, and filling
her Parliament with Generals, each equal, he rhetorically
declares, to Alexander.—But come, my dear fellow," said
I, jumping up, " here have I been holding forth like a
little Socrates, while the day is passing over our heads.
We have forgotten poor Lexilogus, who (I should not
wonder) may have stolen away, like your fox, to Cambridge."

Euphranor, who seemed to linger yet awhile, nevertheless follow'd my example. On looking at my watch
I saw we could not take anything like the walk we had
proposed and yet be at home by their College dinner;†
so as it was I who had wasted the day, I would stand
the expense, I said, of dinner at the Inn; after which we
could all return at our ease to Cambridge in the Evening. As we were leaving the Bowling-green, I called
up to Lycion, who thereupon appeared at the Billiard-
room window with his coat off, and asked him if he had
nearly finish'd his Game? By way of answer, he asked
us if we had done with our Ogres and Giants? whom, on
the contrary, I said, we were now running away from

* *When, says Horace, the Boy of gentle blood, adept enough at feats*
of trivial dexterity, had no seat on the Horse, nor courage to follow
the Hounds— [Substituted for the Latin in final edition.]
† *Then at 3.30 p. m.*

[165]

that we might live to fight another day—would he come
with us into the fields for a walk? or, if he meant to go
on with his Billiards, would he dine with us on our return?
" Not walk with us," he said; and when I spoke of dinner
again, seemed rather to hesitate; but at last said, " Very
well; " and, nodding to us, retired with his cue into the
room.

Then Euphranor and I, leaving the necessary orders
within, return'd a little way to look for Lexilogus, whom
(48) we|soon saw, like a man of honour as he was, coming on
his way to meet us. In less than a minute we had met;
and he apologized for having been delay'd by one of
Aunt Martha's asthma-fits, during which he had not liked
to leave her.

After a brief condolence, we all three turn'd back;
and I told him how, after all, Euphranor and I had play'd
no Billiards, but had been arguing all the time about
Digby and his books.

Lexilogus smiled, but made no remark, being naturally little given to Speech. But the day was delightful,
and we walk'd briskly along the road, conversing on many
topics, till a little further on we got into the fields. These
—for it had been a warm May—were now almost in their
Prime, (and that of the Year, Crabbe used to say, fell
with the mowing,) crop-thick with Daisy, Clover, and
Buttercup; and, as we went along, Euphranor, whose
thoughts still ran on what we had been talking about,
quoted from Chaucer whom we had lately been looking
at together:

"Embrouded was he as it were a Mede,
  Alle ful of fresshe Floures, white and rede,"

and added, " What a picture was that, by the way, of a young Knight! "

I had half-forgotten the passage, and Lexilogus had never read Chaucer: so I begg'd Euphranor to repeat it; which he did, with an occasional pause in his Memory, and jog from mine.

' With him ther was his Sone, a yonge Squier,
  A Lover, and a lusty Bacheler,
  With Lockes crull, as they were laide in presse;
  Of Twenty yere of age he was, I gesse;
  Of his Stature he was of even lengthe,   *(49)*
  And wonderly deliver, and grete of Strengthe;
  And he hadde be somtime in Chevachie,
  In Flaundres, in Artois, and in Picardie,
  And borne him wel, as of so litel space,
  In hope to stonden in his Ladies grace.
  Embrouded was he as it were a Mede,
  Alle ful of fresshe Floures, white and rede;
  Singing he was, or floyting alle the day;
  He was as fresshe as is the moneth of May:
  Short was his Goune with sleves long and wide,
  Wel coude he sitte on Hors, and fayre ride,
  He coude Songes make, and well endite,
  Juste, and eke dance, and wel pourtraie and write.
  So hote he loved that by nightertale
  He slep no more than doth the Nightingale.
  Curteis he was, lowly, and servisable,
  And carf before his Fader at the table.'

[167   ]

" Chaucer, however," said Euphranor, when he had
finished the passage, " credited his young Squire with
other Accomplishments than you would trust him with,
Doctor. See, he dances, draws, and even indites songs
—somewhat of a Dilettante, after all."

" But also," I added, " is ' grete of Strengthe,' ' coude
fayre ride,' having already ' borne him wel in Chevachie.'
Besides," continued I, (who had not yet subsided, I suppose, from the long swell of my former sententiousness,)
" in those days, you know, there was scarce any Reading,
which now, for better or worse, occupies so much of our
time; Men left that to Clerk and Schoolman; contented,
as we before agreed, to follow their bidding to Pilgrimage and Holy war. Some of those gentler Accomplishments may then have been needed to soften manners,
just as rougher ones to strengthen ours. And, long after
that, Sir Philip Sidney might well indulge in a little Son-
(50) |neteering, amid all those public services which ended at
Zutfen; as later on, in the Stuart days, Lord Dorset troll
off—' *To all you Ladies now on Land,*' from the Fleet
that was just going into Action off the coast of Holland."

" Even Master Samuel Pepys," said Euphranor, laughing, " might sit with a good grace down to practise his
' *Beauty retire,*' after riding to Huntingdon and back,
as might Parson Adams have done many years after."

" They were both prefigured among those Canterbury
Pilgrims so many years before," said I. " Only think
of it! Some nine-and-twenty, I think, ' by aventure
yfalle in feleweship,' High and Low, Rich and Poor,

[168]

Saint and Sinner, Cleric and Lay, Knight, Ploughman, Prioress, Wife of Bath, Shipman, hunting Abbot-like Monk, Poor Parson—(Adams' Progenitor)—Webster (Pepys')—on rough-riding ' Stot ' or ambling Palfrey, marshall'd by mine Host of the Tabard to the music of the Miller's Bag-pipes, on their sacred errand to St. Thomas'; and one among them taking note of all in Verse still fresh as the air of those Kentish hills they travelled over on that April morning four hundred years ago."

" Lydgate too, I remember," said Euphranor, " tells of Chaucer's good-humour'd encouragement of his Brother-poets—I cannot now recollect the lines," he added, after pausing a little.*

" A famous Man of Business too," said I, " employ'd (51) by Princes at home and abroad. And ready to fight as to write; having, he says, when some City people had accused him of Untruth, ' prepared his body for Mars his doing, if any contraried his saws.' "

"A Poet after your own heart, Doctor, sound in wind and limb, Mind and Body. In general, however, they are said to be a sickly, irritable, inactive, and solitary race."

" Not our 'Canterbury Pilgrim ' for one," said I; " no,

---

* The verses Euphranor could not remember are these:

" For Chaucer that my Master was, and knew
What did belong to writing Verse and Prose,
Ne'er stumbled at small faults, nor yet did view
With scornful eyes the works and books of those
That in his time did write, nor yet would taunt
At any man, to fear him or to daunt."

[169]

nor his successor, William Shakespeare, who, after a somewhat roving Knighthood in the country, became a Player, Play-wright, and Play-manager in London, where, after managing (as not all managers do) to make a sufficient fortune, he returned home again to settle in his native Stratford—whither by the way he had made occasional Pilgrimages before—on horseback, of course— putting up—for the night—at the Angel of Oxford— about which some stories are told——"

" As fabulous as probably those of his poaching in earlier days," said Euphranor.

" Well, however that may be—and I constantly believe in the poaching part of the Story—to Stratford he finally retired, where he built a house, and planted Mulberries, and kept company with John-a-Combe, and the neigh- bouring Knights and Squires—except perhaps the Lucys —as merrily as with the Wits of London; all the while supplying his own little 'Globe '—and, from it, ' the Great globe itself,' with certain manuscripts, in which (say his Fellow-players and first Editors) Head and hand went so easily together as scarce to leave a blot on the pages they travell'd over."

" Somewhat resembling Sir Walter Scott's, I think," said Euphranor, " in that love for Country home, and
(52) Country|neighbour—aye, and somewhat also in that easy intercourse between Head and hand in composition which those who knew them tell of—however unequal in the result. Do you remember Lockhart's saying how glibly

[170]

Sir Walter's pen was heard to canter over the paper, before ' Atra Cura ' saddled herself behind him? "

" Ah, yes," said I; " ' Magician of the North ' they
call'd him in my own boyish days; and such he is to me
now; though maybe not an Archi-magus like him of
Stratford, to set me down in Rome, Athens, Egypt, with
their Heroes, Heroines, and Commoners, moving and
talking as living men and women about me, howsoever
' larger than human ' through the breath of Imagination
in which he has clothed them."

" Somebody—your Carlyle, I believe," said Euphranor, " lays it down that Sir Walter's Characters are in
general fashioned from without to within—the reverse
of Shakespeare's way—and Nature's."

" What," said I, " according to old Sartor's theory,
beginning from the over-coat of temporary Circumstance,
through the temporary Tailor's ' Just-au-corps,' till arriv-
ing at such centre of Humanity as may lie within the
bodily jerkin we talk'd of? "

" Something of that sort, I suppose," said Euphranor;
" but an you love me, Doctor, no more of that odious old
jerkin, whether Sterne's or Carlyle's."

" Well," said I, " if the Sartor's charge hold good, it
must lie against the Heroes and Heroines of the later,
half-historical, Romances; in which, nevertheless, are
scenes where our Elizabeth, and James, and Lewis of
France figure, that seem to me as good in Character and
Circumstance as any in that Henry the Eighth, which

[171]

(53) has always till quite|lately been accepted for Shake-
speare's. But Sartor's self will hardly maintain his charge
against the Deanses, Dumbiedykes, Ochiltrees, Baillies,
and others of the bonâ-fide *Scotch* Novels, with the likes
of whom Scott fell ' in feleweship ' from a Boy, riding
about the country—' born to be a trooper,' he said of
himself; no, nor with the Bradwardines, Bothwells,
Maccombicks, Macbriars, and others, Highlander, Low-
lander, Royalist, Roundhead, Churchman or Covenanter,
whom he animated with the true Scottish blood which
ran in himself as well as in those he lived among, and so
peopled those stories which are become Household History to us. I declare that I scarce know whether
Macbeth's blasted heath would move me more than
did the first sight of the Lammermoor Hills when I
rounded the Scottish coast on first going to Edinburgh;
or of that ancient ' Heart of Mid-Lothian ' when I got
there. But the domestic Tragedy naturally comes more
nearly home to the bosom of your Philistine."

" Sir Walter's stately neighbour across the Tweed,"
said Euphranor, " took no great account of his Novels,
and none at all of his Verse—though, by the way, he did
call him 'Great Minstrel of the Border ' after revisiting
Yarrow in his company; perhaps he meant it only of
the Minstrelsy which Scott collected, you know."

" Wordsworth? " said I—" a man of the Milton rather
than of the Chaucer and Shakespeare type—without
humour, like the rest of his Brethren of the Lake."

" Not but he loves Chaucer as much as you can, Doctor, for those fresh touches of Nature, and tenderness of Heart—insomuch that he has re-cast the Jew of Lincoln's Story into a form more available for modern readers."

" And successfully? "

" Ask Lexilogus—Ah! I forget that he never read *(54)* Chaucer; but I know that he loves Wordsworth next to his own Cowper."

Lexilogus believed that he liked the Poem in question, but he was not so familiar with it as with many other of Wordsworth's pieces.

" Ah, you and I, Euphranor," said I, " must one day teach Lexilogus the original before he is become too great a Don to heed such matters."

Lexilogus smiled, and Euphranor said that before that time came Lexilogus and he would teach me in return to love Wordsworth more than I did—or pretended to do. Not only the Poet, but the Man, he said, who loved his Home as well as Shakespeare and Scott loved theirs— aye, and his Country Neighbours too, though perhaps in a sedater way; and, as so many of his Poems show, as sensible as Sir Walter of the sterling virtues of the Moun- taineers and Dalesmen he lived among, though, maybe, not of their humour.

" Was he not also pretty exact in his office of stamp- distributor among them? " asked I.

" Come, you must not quarrel, Doctor, with the Busi- ness which, as with Chaucer and Shakespeare, may have kept the Poetic Element in due proportion with the rest —including, by the way, such a store of your Animal,

[173]

laid in from constant climbing the mountain, and skating on the lake, that he may still be seen, I am told, at near upon Eighty, travelling with the shadow of the cloud up Helvellyn."

"Bravo, Old Man of the Mountains!" said I. "But, nevertheless, it would not have been amiss with him had he been sent earlier, and further, from his mountain-mother's lap, and had some of his—conceit, I (55) |must not call it—Pride, then—taken out of him by a freer intercourse with men."

"I suppose," said Euphranor, again laughing, "you would knock a young Apollo about like the rest of us common pottery?"

"I think I *should* send young Wordsworth to that Military Drill of ours, and see if some rough-riding would not draw some of that dangerous Sensibility which 'young Edwin' is apt to mistake for poetical Genius."

"Gray had more than that in him, I know," said Euphranor; "but I doubt what might have become of his poetry had such been the discipline of his Eton day."

"Perhaps something better—perhaps nothing at all— and *he* the happier man."

"But not *you,* Doctor—for the loss of his Elegy— with all your talk."

"No; I am always remembering, and always forgetting it; remembering, I mean, the several stanzas, and forgetting how they link together; partly, perhaps, because of each being so severally elaborated. Neither

Yeomanry Drill—nor daily Plough—drove the Muse out of Burns."

" Nor the Melancholy neither, for that matter," said Euphranor. " Those ' Banks and braes ' of his could not bestow on him even the ' momentary joy ' which those Eton fields ' beloved in vain ' breathed into the heart of Gray."

" Are you not forgetting," said I, " that Burns was not then singing of himself, but of some forsaken damsel, as appears by the second stanza, which few, by the way, care to remember? As unremember'd it may have been," I continued, after a pause, " by the only living— and like to live—Poet I had known, when, so many years after, he found himself beside that ' bonnie Doon ' and— whether it|were from recollection of poor Burns, or of (56) ' the days that are no more ' which haunt us all, I know not—I think he did not know—but, he somehow ' broke,' as he told me, ' broke into a passion of tears '—Of tears which, during a pretty long and intimate intercourse, I had never seen glisten in his eye but once, when reading Virgil—' dear old Virgil,' as he call'd him—together: and then of the burning of Troy in the Second Æneid— whether moved by the catastrophe's self, or the majesty of the Verse it is told in—or, as before, scarce knowing why. For, as King Arthur shall bear witness, no young Edwin he, though, as a great Poet, comprehending all the softer stops of human Emotion in that Diapason* where the Intellectual, no less than what is call'd the Poetical, faculty

* 'Register' for 'Diapason' in final edition.

EUPHRANOR.

predominated. As all who knew him know, a Man at
all points, Euphranor—like your Digby, of grand proportion and feature, significant of that inward Chivalry,
becoming his ancient and honourable race; when himself
a 'Yonge Squier,' like him in Chaucer 'grete of strengthe,'
that could hurl the crow-bar further than any of the neighbouring clowns, whose humours, as well as of their bet-
ters,—Knight, Squire, Landlord and Land-tenant,—he
took quiet note of, like Chaucer himself. Like your
Wordsworth on the Mountain, he too, when a Lad, abroad
on the Wold; sometimes of a night with the Shepherd;
watching not only the Sheep* on the greensward, whom
individually he knew, but also

> 'The fleecy Star that bears
> Andromeda far off Atlantic seas'

along with those other Zodiacal constellations which Aries,
I think, leads over the field of Heaven. He then observed also some of those uncertain phenomena of Night:
(57) unsur-|mised apparitions of the Northern Aurora, by
some shy glimpses of which no winter—no, nor even summer—night, he said, was utterly unvisited; and those
strange voices, whether of creeping brook, or copses muttering to themselves far off—perhaps the yet more im-
possible Sea—together with 'other sounds we know
not whence they come,' says Crabbe, but all inaudible to
the ear of Day. He was not then, I suppose, unless the
Word spontaneously came upon him, thinking how to

* 'Flock' for 'Sheep,' in final edition.

[176]

turn what he saw and heard into Verse; a premeditation that is very likely to defeat itself.* For is not what we call *Poetry* said to be an Inspiration, which, if not kindling at the sudden collision, or recollection, of Reality, will yet less be quicken'd by anticipation, howsoever it may be controll'd by afterthought?"

Something to this effect I said, though, were it but for lack of walking breath, at no so long-winded a flight † of eloquence. And then Euphranor, whose lungs were in so much better order than mine, though I had left him so little opportunity for using them, took up where I left off, and partly read, and partly told us of a delightful passage from his .Godefridus, to this effect, that, if the Poet could not invent, neither could his Reader understand him, when he told of Ulysses and Diomed listening to the crane clanging in the marsh by night, without having *experienced* something of the sort. And so we went on, partly in jest, partly in earnest, drawing Philosophers of all kinds into the same net in which we had entangled the Poet and his Critic—How the Moralist who worked alone in his closet was apt to mismeasure Humanity, and be very angry when the cloth he cut out for him would not fit—how the best Histories were written by those who themselves had been actors in them—Gibbon, one of the next best, I|believe, recording how the discipline of the (58)

---

* *"Previously breathing, as it were, upon the mirror which is to receive the Image that most assuredly flashes Reality into words."*— Paragraph so ends in final edition.
† 'Stretch' for 'flight,' in final edition.

[177]

EUPHRANOR.

Hampshire Militia he served as Captain in—how odd he must have looked in the uniform!—enlighten'd him as to the evolutions of a Roman Legion—And so on a great deal more; till, suddenly observing how the sun had declined from his meridian, I look'd at my watch, and ask'd my companions did not they begin to feel hungry, like myself? They agreed with me; and we turn'd homeward: and as Lexilogus had hitherto borne so little part in the conversation, I began to question him about Herodotus and Strabo, (whose books I had seen lying open upon his table,) and drew from him some information about the courses of the Nile and the Danube, and the Geography of the Old World: till, all of a sudden, our conversation skipt from Olympus, I think, to the hills of Yorkshire —our own old hills—and the old friends and neighbours who dwelt among them. And as we were thus talking, we heard the galloping of Horses behind us, (for we were now again upon the main road,) and, looking back as they were just coming up, I recognised Phidippus for one of the riders, with two others whom I did not know. I held up my hand, and call'd out to him as he was passing; and Phidippus, drawing up his Horse all snorting and agitated with her arrested course, wheel'd back and came along-side of us.

I ask'd him what he was about, galloping along the road; I thought scientific men were more tender of their horses' legs and feet. But the roads, he said, were quite soft with the late rains; and they were only trying each other's speed for a mile or so.

By this time his two companions had pulled up some

way forward, and were calling him to come on; but he said, laughing, " they had quite enough of it," and ad-
|dress'd himself with many a " Steady!" and " So! So!" *(59)*
to pacify Miss Middleton, as he called her, who still caper'd, plung'd, and snatch'd at her bridle; his friends shouting louder and louder—" Why the Devil he didn't come on?"

He waved his hand to them in return; and with a " Confound " and " Deuce take the Fellow," they set off away toward the town. On which Miss Middleton began afresh, plunging, and blowing out a peony nostril after her flying fellows; until, what with their dwindling in distance, and some expostulation address'd to her by her Master as to a fractious Child, she seem'd to make up her mind to the indignity, and composed herself to go pretty quietly beside us.

I then asked him did he not remember Lexilogus,— (Euphranor he had already recognised,)—and Phidippus, who really had not hitherto seen who it was, (Lexilogus looking shyly down all the while,) call'd out heartily to him, and, wheeling his mare suddenly behind us, took hold of his hand, and began to inquire about his family in Yorkshire.

" One would suppose," said I, " you two fellows had not met for years."

" It was true," Phidippus said, " they did not meet as often as he wish'd; but Lexilogus would not come to his rooms, and he did not like to disturb Lexilogus at his books; and so the time went on."

I then inquired about his own reading, which, though

not much, was not utterly neglected, it seemed; and he said he had meant to ask one of us to beat something into his stupid head this summer in Yorkshire.

Lexilogus, I knew, meant to stop at Cambridge all the long Vacation; but Euphranor said he should be at home, for anything he then knew, and they could talk the mat- (60) ter|over when the time came. We then again fell to talking of our County; and among other things I asked Phidippus if his horse were Yorkshire,—of old famous for its breed, as well as of Riders,—and how long he had her, and so forth.

Yorkshire she was, a present from his Father, " and a great pet," he said, bending down his head, which Miss Middleton answered by a dip of hers, shaking the bit in her mouth, and breaking into a little canter, which however was easily suppress'd.

" Miss Middleton? " said I—" what, by Bay Middleton out of Coquette, by Tomboy out of High-Life Below-Stairs, right up to Mahomet and his Mares? "

" Right," he answered, laughing, " as far as Bay Middleton was concerned."

" But, Phidippus," said I, " she's as black as a coal! "

" And so was her Dam, a Yorkshire Mare," he answered; which, I said, saved the credit of all parties. Might she perhaps be descended from our famous " Yorkshire Jenny," renowned in Newmarket Verse? But Phidippus had never heard of " Yorkshire Jenny," nor of the Ballad, which I promised to acquaint him with, if

he would stop on his way back, and dine with us at Chesterton, where his Mare might have her Dinner too—all
of us Yorkshiremen except Lycion, whom he knew a little
of. There was to be a Boat-race, however, in the evening, which Phidippus said he must leave us to attend, if
dine with us he did; for, though not one of the Crew on
this occasion, (not being one of the best,) he must yet see
his own Trinity boat keep the head of the River. As
to that, I said, we were all bound the same way, which
indeed Euphranor had proposed before; and so the whole
affair was settled.

As we went along, I began questioning him concerning
|some of those Equestrian difficulties which Euphranor (61)
and I had been talking of: all which Phidippus thought
was only my usual banter—" he was no Judge—I must
ask older hands," and so forth—until we reach'd the Inn,
when I begg'd Euphranor to order dinner at once, while
I and Lexilogus accompanied Phidippus to the Stable.
There, after giving his mare in charge to the hostler with
due directions as to her toilet and table, he took off her
saddle and bridle himself, and adjusted the head-stall.
Then, follow'd out of the stable by her flaming eye and
pointed ears, he too pausing a moment on the threshold
to ask me " was she not a Beauty? " (for he persisted in
the delusion of my knowing more of the matter than I
chose to confess,) we cross'd over into the house.

There, having wash'd our hands and faces, we went
up into the Billiard-room, where we found Euphranor and
Lycion playing,—Lycion very lazily, like a man who had

THIRD
EDITION

EUPHRANOR.

already too much of it, but yet nothing better to do. After a short while, the girl came to tell us all was ready; and, after that slight hesitation as to precedence which Englishmen rarely forget on the least ceremonious occasions,—Lexilogus, in particular, pausing timidly at the door, and Euphranor pushing him gently forward,—we got down to the little Parlour, very airy and pleasant, with its windows opening on the bowling-green, the table laid with a clean white cloth, and upon that a dish of smoking beef-steak, at which I, as master of the Feast, and, as Euphranor slyly intimated, otherwise entitled, sat down to officiate. For some time the clatter of knife and fork, and the pouring of ale, went on, mix'd with some conversation among the young men about College matters: till Lycion began to tell us of a gay Ball he *(62)* had lately been at, and of the Families|there; among whom he named three young Ladies from a neighbouring County, by far the handsomest women present, he said.

" And very accomplish'd, too, I am told," said Euphranor.

" Oh, as for that," replied Lycion, " they *Valse* very well." He hated " your accomplished women," he said.

" Well, there," said Euphranor, " I suppose the Doctor will agree with you."

I said, certainly *Valsing* would be no great use to me personally—unless, as some Lady of equal size and greater rank had said, I could meet with a concave partner.

[182]

" One knows so exactly," said Lycion, " what the Doctor would choose,—a woman

'Well versed in the Arts
Of Pies, Puddings, and Tarts,'

as one used to read of somewhere, I remember."

" Not forgetting," said I, " the being able to help in
compounding a pill or a plaister; which I dare say your
Great-grandmother knew something about, Lycion, for
in those days, you know, Great ladies studied Simples.
Well, so I am fitted,—as Lycion is to be with one who
can *Valse* through life with him."

" 'And follow so the ever-rolling Year
With profitable labour to their graves,' "

added Euphranor, laughing.

" I don't want to marry her," said Lycion testily.

" Then Euphranor," said I, " will advertise for a
' Strong-minded ' Female, able to read Plato with him,
and Wordsworth, and Digby, and become a Mother of
Heroes. As to Phidippus there is no doubt—Diana
Vernon—"

But Phidippus disclaimed any taste for Sporting
ladies.

" Well, come," said I, passing round a bottle of sherry *(63)*
I had just call'd for, " every man to his liking, only all
of you taking care to secure the accomplishments of
Health and Good-humour."

" Ah, there it is, out at last!" cried Euphranor, clap-

[183]

ping his hands; " I knew the Doctor would choose for
us as Frederic for his Grenadiers."

" So you may accommodate me," said I, " with a motto
from another old Song whenever my time comes;

'Give Isaac the Nymph who no beauty can boast,
But Health and Good-humour to make her his toast.'

Well, every man to his fancy—Here's to mine!—And
when we have finish'd the bottle, which seems about equal
to one more errand round the table, we will adjourn, if
you like, to the Bowling-green, which Euphranor will
tell us was the goodly custom of our Forefathers, and I
can recommend as a very wholesome after-dinner exercise."

" Not, however, till we have the Doctor's famous Ballad
about Miss Middleton's possible Great-Great-Grand-
mother," cried Euphranor, " by way of Pindaric close to
this Heroic entertainment, sung from the Chair, who
probably composed it——"

"As little as could sing it," I assured him.

" Oh, I remember, it was the Jockey who rode her! "

" Perhaps only his Helper," answered I; " such bad
grammar, and rhyme, and altogether want of what your
man—how do you call him—G.O.E.T.H.E.—'Gewty,' will
that do?—calls, I believe, *Art.*"

"Who nevertheless maintained,"*said Euphranor,"that
the Ballad was scarcely possible but to those who simply
saw with their Eyes, heard with their Ears—and, I really

* 'Once declares' for 'maintained,' in final edition.

[184]

think he said, fought with their fists,—I suppose also felt *(64)* with their hearts—without any notion of *'Art'*—although Goethe himself, Schiller, and Rückert, and other of your æsthetic Germans, Doctor, have latterly done best in that line, I believe."

"Better than Cowper's 'Royal George,'" said I, "where every word of the narrative *tells,* as from a Seaman's lips?"

"*That* is something before our time, Doctor."

"Better then than some of Campbell's which follow'd it? or some of Sir Walter's? or 'The Lord of Burleigh,' which is later than all? But enough that my poor Jock may chance to sing of his Mare as well as Shenstone of his Strephon and Delia."

"Or more modern Bards of Cocles in the Tiber, or Regulus in the Tub," said Euphranor. — "But come! Song from the Chair!" he call'd out, tapping his glass on the table, which Phidippus echoed with his.

So with a prelusive "Well then," I began—

"'I'll sing you a Song, and a merry, merry Song'—

By the way, Phidippus, what an odd notion of merriment is a Jockey's, if this Song be a sample. I think I have observed they have grave, taciturn faces, especially when old, which they soon get to look. Is this from much wasting, to carry little Flesh—and large—Responsibility?"

"Doctor, Doctor, leave your—faces, and begin!" interrupted Euphranor. "I must call the Chair to Order."

[185]

EUPHRANOR.

Thus admonish'd, with some slight interpolations, (to be jump'd by the Æsthetic,) I repeated the poor Ballad which, dropt I know not how nor when into my ear, had managed, as others we had talk'd of, to chink itself in some corner of a memory that should have been occupied with other professional jargon than a " Jockey's."

(65)

I.

"I'll sing you a Song, and a merry, merry Song,
        Concerning our Yorkshire Jen;
Who never yet ran with Horse or Mare,
        That ever she cared for a pin.

II.

When first she came to Newmarket town,
        The Sportsmen all view'd her around;
All the cry was, 'Alas, poor wench,
        Thou never can run this ground!'

III.

When they came to the starting-post,
        The Mare look'd very smart;
And let them all say what they will,
        She never lost her start—

—which I don't quite understand, by the way: do you, Lycion?"—No answer.

IV.

"When they got to the Two-mile post,
        Poor Jenny was cast behind:
She was cast behind, she was cast behind,
        All for to take her wind.

[186]

V.

When they got to the Three-mile post,
The Mare look'd very pale—

(Phidippus! "—His knee moved under the table—)

"She laid down her ears on her bonny neck,
And by them all did she sail;

VI.   (*Accelerando.*)

'Come follow me, come follow me,
All you who run so neat;
And ere that you catch me again,
I'll make you well to sweat.'

VII.   (*Grandioso.*)   (66)

When she got to the Winning-post,
The people all gave a shout:
And Jenny click'd up her Lily-white foot,
And jump'd like any Buck.

VIII.

The Jockey said to her, 'This race you have run.
This race for me you have got;
You could gallop it all over again,
When the rest could hardly trot!'"

" They were Four-mile Heats in those days, you see,
would pose your modern Middletons, though Miss Jenny,
laying back her ears—away from catching the Wind,

some think—and otherwise *'pale,'* with the distended vein
and starting sinew of that Three-mile crisis, nevertheless,
on coming triumphantly in, click'd up that lily-white foot
of hers, (of which *one,* I have heard say, is as good a sign
as all four white are a bad,) and could, as the Jockey
thought, have gallop'd it all over again—Can't you see
him, Phidippus, for once forgetful of his professional
stoicism, (but I don't think Jockeys were quite so politic
then,) bending forward to pat the bonny Neck that measured the Victory, as he rides her slowly back to the—
Weighing-house, is it?—follow'd by the scarlet-coated
Horsemen and shouting People of those days?—all silent,
and pass'd away for ever now, unless from the memory
of one pursy Doctor, who, were she but alive, would
hardly know Jenny's head from her tail—And now will
you have any more wine?" said I, holding up the empty
decanter.

Phidippus, hastily finishing his glass, jump'd up; and,
the others following him with more or less alacrity, we
all sallied forth on the Bowling-green.   As soon as there,
(67) |Lycion of course pull'd out his Cigar-case, (which he
had eyed, I saw, with really good-humoured resignation
during the Ballad,) and offer'd it all round, telling
Phidippus he could recommend the contents as some of
Pontet's best.   But Phidippus did not smoke, he said;
which, together with his declining to bet on the Boat-race,
caused Lycion, I thought, to look on him with some in-
dulgence.

And now Jack was rolled upon the green; and I bowl'd

[188   ]

after him first, pretty well; then Euphranor still better; then Lycion, with great indifference and indifferent success; then Phidippus, who about rivall'd me; and last of all, Lexilogus, whom Phidippus had been instructing in the mystery of the bias with some little side-rolls along the turf, and who, he said, only wanted a little practice to play as well as the best of us.

Meanwhile, the shadows lengthen'd along the grass, and after several bouts of play, Phidippus, who had to ride round by Cambridge, said he must be off in time to see his friends start. We should soon follow, I said; and Euphranor asked him to his rooms after the race. But Phidippus was engaged to sup with his crew.

" Where you will all be drunk," said I.

" No; there," said he, " you are quite mistaken, Doctor."

" Well, well," I said, " away, then, to your race and your supper."

" 'Μετὰ σώφρονος ἡλικιώτου,' " added Euphranor, smiling.

" Μετὰ, 'with,' or 'after,' " said Phidippus, putting on his gloves.

" Well, go on, Sir," said I, " Σώφρονος? "

" A temperate—something or other—"

" Ἡλικιωτου ? "

" Supper?"—he hesitated, smiling—" 'After a temper- (68) ate supper?' "

" Go down, Sir; go down this instant!" I roar'd out to him as he ran from the bowling-green. And in a few minutes we heard his mare's feet shuffling over the stable threshold, and directly afterwards breaking into a retreating canter beyond.

Shortly after this, the rest of us agreed it was time to be gone. We walk'd along the fields by the Church, (purposely to ask about the sick Lady by the way,) cross'd the Ferry, and mingled with the crowd upon the opposite shore; Townsmen and Gownsmen, with the tassell'd Fellow-commoner sprinkled here and there—Reading men and Sporting men—Fellows, and even Masters of Colleges, not indifferent to the prowess of their respective Crews—all these, conversing on all sorts of topics, from the slang in *Bell's Life* to the last new German Revelation, and moving in ever-changing groups down the shore of the river, at whose farther bend was a little knot of Ladies gathered up on a green knoll faced and illuminated by the beams of the setting sun. Beyond which point was at length heard some indistinct shouting, which gradually increased, until " They are off—they are coming! " suspended other conversation among ourselves; and suddenly the head of the first boat turn'd the corner; and then another close upon it; and then a third; the crews pulling with all their might compacted into perfect rhythm; and the crowd on shore turning round to follow along with them, waving hats and caps, and cheering, " Bravo, St. John's! " " Go it, Trinity! "—the high crest and blowing forelock of Phidippus's mare, and he himself shouting encouragement to his crew, conspicuous over all—until, the boats reaching us, we also were caught
(69) up in|the returning tide of spectators, and hurried back

[190]

toward the goal; where we arrived just in time to see the Ensign of Trinity lowered from its pride of place, and the Eagle of St. John's soaring there instead. Then, waiting a little while to hear how the winner had won, and the loser lost, and watching Phidippus engaged in eager conversation with his defeated brethren, I took Euphranor and Lexilogus under either arm (Lycion having got into better company elsewhere,) and walk'd home with them across the meadow leading to the town, whither the dusky troops of Gownsmen with all their confused voices seem'd as it were evaporating in the twilight, while a Nightingale began to be heard among the flowering Chestnuts of Jesus.

FINIS.

EXTRACTS FROM FITZGERALD'S LETTERS RELATING TO "AGAMEMNON" SECOND EDITION.

To Fanny Kemble.

[Lowestoft, April, 1876.]

. . . *Quaritch has begun to print Agamemnon now—so leisurely that I fancy he wishes to wait till the old Persian is exhausted, and so join the two. I certainly am in no hurry; for I fully believe we shall only get abused for the Greek in proportion as we were praised for the Persian—in England, I mean: for you have made America more favourable.*

To Fanny Kemble.

Woodbridge: July 31, 1876.

. . . *I shall send you Quaritch's Reprint of 'Agamemnon': which is just done after many blunders. The revises were not sent me, as I desired: so several things are left as I meant not: but 'enfin' here it is at last so fine that I am ashamed of it. For, whatever the merit of it may be, it can't come near all this fine Paper, Margin, etc., which Quaritch will have as counting on only a few buyers, who will buy—in America almost wholly, I think —And, as this is wholly due to you, I send you the Reprint, however little different to what you had before.*

To Mrs. Cowell.

12 Marine Terrace, Lowestoft, March 11, '77.

. . . *If the Pall Mall Critic knew Greek, I am rather surprised he should have vouchsafed even so much praise as the words you quoted. But I certainly have found that those few whom I meant it for, not Greek scholars, have been more interested in it than I expected.* . . .

To Fanny Kemble.

[June, 1877.]

. . . .

I think I never told you—what is the fact, however— that I had wished to dedicate Agamemnon to you, but thought I could not do so without my own name appended. Whereas, I could, very simply, as I saw afterwards when too late. If ever he is reprinted I shall (unless you forbid) do as I desired to do: for, if for no other reason, he would probably never have been published but for you. Perhaps, he had better [have] remained in private Life so far as England is concerned.

To C. E. Norton.

Woodbridge, August 21, '77.

. . . *Which leads me to say that some one sent me a number of your American ' Nation ' with a Review of my redoubtable Agamemnon: written by a superior* hand, and, I think, quite discriminating in its distribution of Blame and Praise: though I will not say the Praise was not more than deserved; but it was where deserved, I think.

To C. E. Norton.

Woodbridge, Dec. 15, '78.

. . . Agamemnon haunted me, until I laid his Ghost so far as I myself was concerned. By the way, I see that Dr. Kennedy, Professor of Greek at our Cambridge, has published a Translation of Agamemnon in 'rhythmic English.' So, at any rate, I have been the cause of waking up two great men (Browning and Kennedy) and a minor Third (I forget his name)* to the Trial, if it were only for the purpose of extinguishing my rash attempt. . . .

"Now for a word on FitzGerald's principles of transla-
" tion. The unhappy translator is always being impaled
" on the horns of a dilemma. If he translates literally,
" he produces stuff no mortal can read. . . . If, on
" the other hand, he makes a good and readable thing of
" it, then arise all the people who know the original, and
" begin to peck at it like domestic fowl. If one steers a
" middle course, one pleases nobody. FitzGerald boldly
" adopted the principle that what is wanted in a transla-

* Lord Carnarvon.

" *tion is* this: **To** *give people who don't know the original*
" *a sort of idea of the effect it produces on people who*
" *do.* **For** *this end we must throw all attempt at a* literal
" *translation to the wind.* **We** *must soak ourselves in the*
" *spirit of an author, and reproduce that spirit in as good*
" *poetic style as we may be master of.* **So,** *not only with*
" *Omar, but with his other translations too, he omits whole*
" *passages, puts in bits of his own, modifies and arranges*
" *everything, and makes—a poem.* **It** *is interesting to*
" *compare Paley's translation of the* Agamemnon *of*
" *Æschylus with FitzGerald's from this point of view.*
" *Paley assures us himself, in his Preface (and I suppose*
" *he ought to know), that* his *is readable and tolerably*
" *literal, and then offers us such gems as:* ' *You are some*
" ' *crazy-headed person, or possessed by some god* '; *or,*
" *again,* '*And my inward parts do not vainly bode—the*
" '*heart that whirls in eddies against the midriff, while*
" ' *it justly looks for a fulfilment of its fears.*' *Really, if*
" *Æschylus is that sort of thing, why do we rise up early*
" *and so late take rest that we may proceed B.A. in Arts?*
" **Now** *listen to another bit from FitzGerald, about*
" *Helen's flight from Menelaus:—*

"*Not beside thee in the chamber,*
Menelaus, any more;
But with him she fled with, pillow'd,
On the summer softly-billow'd
Ocean, into dimple wreathing
Underneath a breeze of amber

[xviii]

Air that, as from Eros breathing,
Fill'd the sail and flew before;
Floating on the summer seas
Like some sweet Effigies
Of Eirene's self, or sweeter
Aphrodite, sweeter still:
With the Shepherd, from whose luckless
Hand upon the Phrygian hill,
Of the three Immortals, She
The fatal prize of Beauty bore,
Floating with him o'er the foam
She rose from, to the Shepherd's home
On the Ionian shore."

" *There is hardly a word, hardly a single word of all that*
" *in Æschylus.   But which of the two gives one the im-*
" *pression that Æschylus gives—Paley or FitzGerald?* "

[From a Paper read before the Literary Society of University College, London, on January 24th, 1896, by Arthur Platt, Professor of Greek.]

AGAMEMNON

AGAMEMNON

A TRAGEDY

TAKEN FROM ÆSCHYLUS.

LONDON:

BERNARD QUARITCH,

15 PICCADILLY.

1876.

This Version—or Per-version—of Æschylus was originally printed to be given away among Friends, who either knew nothing of the Original, or would be disposed to excuse the liberties taken with it by an unworthy hand.*

* The second edition (1876) reads "*a less worthy hand:*" and has the following two additional paragraphs :

Such as it is, however, others, whom I do not know, have asked for copies when I had no more copies to give. So Mr. Quaritch ventures on publishing it on his own account, at the risk of facing much less indulgent critics.

I can add little more to the Apology prefixed to the private edition.

PREFACE.

ALL the Choruses in this Tragedy call for a more lyrical Interpreter than myself. But even I might have done better with the first, by mingling fragments of the so oft-told Story, with such dark and ill-ominous presage as would accumulate as Time went on.

So much for the matter. As for the manner; I think that some such form as Tennyson has originated in his version of the Battle of Brunanburh might well be adopted in this case, as in many other of Æschylus' Choruses—such as in the Persæ, the Seven against Thebes, and the Eumenides—the question being whether such a trochaic gallop may not over-ride the Iambic Blank Verse Dialogue that follows it.

I suppose that a literal version of this play, if possible, would scarce be intelligible. Even were the dialogue always clear, the lyric Choruses, which make up so large a part, are so dark and abrupt in themselves, and therefore so much the more mangled and tormented by copyist and commentator, that the most conscientious translator must not only jump at a mean-|ing, but must bridge over a *(iv)* chasm; especially if he determine to complete the antiphony of Strophe and Antistrophe in English verse.

Thus, encumbered with forms which sometimes, I

think, hang heavy on Æschylus himself;[1] struggling with indistinct meanings, obscure allusions, and even with *puns* which some have tried to reproduce in English; this grand play, which to the scholar and the poet, lives, breathes, and moves in the dead language, has hitherto seemed to me to drag and stifle under conscientious translation into the living; that is to say, to have lost that which I think the drama can least afford to lose all the world over. And so it was that, hopeless of succeeding where as good versifiers, and better scholars, seemed to me to have failed, I came first to break the bounds of Greek Tragedy; then to swerve from the Master's footsteps;

(v) and so, one|license drawing on another to make all of a piece, arrived at the present anomalous conclusion. If it has succeeded in shaping itself into a distinct, consistent and animated Whole, through which the reader can follow without halting, and not without accelerating interest from beginning to end, he will perhaps excuse my acknowledged transgressions,* and will not disdain the Jade that has carried him so far so well till he find himself mounted on a Thorough-bred whose thunder-clothed neck and long-resounding pace shall better keep up with the Original.

For to re-create the Tragedy, body and soul, into English, and make the Poet free of the language which reigns

---

[1] *For instance, the long antiphonal dialogue of the Chorus debating what to do—or whether do anything—after hearing their master twice cry out (in pure Iambics also) that he is murdered.*

* *In the edition of 1876 this sentence ends thus,—unless as well or better satisfied by some more faithful Interpreter, or by one more entitled than myself to make free with the Original.*

over that half of the world never dreamt of in his philosophy, must be reserved—especially the Lyric part—for
some Poet, worthy of that name, and of congenial
Genius with the Greek. Would that every one such would *(vi)*
devote himself to one such work! whether by Translation,
Paraphrase, or Metaphrase, to use Dryden's definition,
whose Alexander's Feast, and|some fragments of whose
Plays, indicate that he, perhaps, might have rendered
such a service to Æschylus and to us. Or, to go further
back in our own Drama, one thinks what Marlowe might
have done; himself a translator from the Greek; something akin to Æschylus in his genius; still more in his
grandiose, and sometimes *authadostomous* verse; of which
some lines relating to this very play fall so little short of
Greek, that I shall but shame my own by quoting them
before hand;

> "Is this the face that launch'd a thousand ships,
> And burnt the topless towers of Ilium?
> Sweet Helen, make me immortal with a kiss!"

[199]

DRAMATIS PERSONÆ.

AGAMEMNON, *King of Argos.*

CLYTEMNESTRA, *his Queen.*

ÆGISTHUS, *his Cousin.*

CASSANDRA, *Daughter of King* PRIAM.

HERALD.

CHORUS *of ancient Councillors.*

The scene is at ARGOS.

AGAMEMNON.

[AGAMEMNON's *Palace: a Warder on the Battlements.*]

WARDER.

[Once more, once more, and once again once more]
I crave the Gods' compassion, and release
From this inexorable watch, that now
For one whole year, close as a couching dog,
On Agamemnon's housetop have I kept,
Contemplating the muster of the stars
And those transplendent Dynasties of Heav'n [1]
That, as alternately they rise and fall,
Draw Warmth and Winter over mortal man.
Thus, and thus long, I say, at the behest   *(2)*
Of the man-minded Woman who here rules,
Here have I watch'd till yonder mountain-top
Shall kindle with a signal-light from Troy.
And watch'd in vain, couch'd on the barren stone,
Night after night, night after night, alone,
Ev'n by a wandering dream unvisited,

---

[1] *The commentators generally understand these* λαμπροὺς δυνάστας
*to mean Sun and Moon. Blomfield, I believe, admits they may be the
Constellations by which the seasons were anciently marked, as in the
case of the Pleiades further on in the Play. The Moon, I suppose,
had no part to play in such a computation; and, as for the Sun, the
beacon-fire surely implies a night-watch.*

AGAMEMNON.

To which the terror of my post denies
The customary passage of closed eyes.
From which, when haply nodding, I would scare
Forbidden sleep, or charm long night away
With some old ballad of the good old times,
The foolish song falls presently to tears,
Remembering the glories of this House,
Where all is not as all was wont to be,—
No, nor as should—Alas, these royal walls,
Had they but tongue (as ears and eyes, men say)
Would tell strange stories!—But, for fear they should,
Mine shall be mute as they are.   Only this—
And this no treason surely—might I but,
But once more might I, see my lord again
Safe home!   But once more look upon his face!
But once more take his hand in mine!—

Hilloa!

(3) The words scarce from my lips—Have the Gods heard?
Or am I dreaming wide awake? as wide
Awake I am—The Light!   The Light!   The Light!
Long look'd for, long despair'd of, on the Height!
Oh more to me than all the stars of night!
More than the Morning-star!—more than the Sun
Who breaks my nightly watch, this rising one
Which tells me that my year-long night is done!
When, shaking off the collar of my watch,

I first to Clytemnestra shall report
Such news as, if indeed a lucky cast
For her and Argos, sure a Main to me!
But grant the Gods, to all!   A master-cast,
More than compensating all losses past;
And lighting up our altars with a fire
Of Victory that never shall expire!

    [*Exit Warder.   Daylight gradually dawns,*
             and enter slowly Chorus.

CHORUS.

I.

ANOTHER rising of the sun
   That rolls another year away,
Sees us through the portal dun
   Dividing night and day
Like to phantoms from the crypt   *(4)*
Of Morpheus or of Hades slipt,
   Through the sleeping city creeping,
Murmuring an ancient song
Of unvindicated wrong,
Ten year told as ten year long
Since to revenge the great abuse
   To Themis done by Priam's son,
The Brother-Princes that, co-heir
Of Athens, share his royal chair,

And from the authentic hand of Zeus
His delegated sceptre bear,
  Startled Greece with such a cry
For Vengeance as a plunder'd pair
Of Eagles over their aerial lair
Screaming, to whirlpool lash the waves of air.

II.

THE Robber, blinded in his own conceit,
    Must needs think Retribution deaf and blind.
    Fool! not to know what tongue was in the wind,
When Tellus shudder'd under flying feet,
    When stricken Ocean under alien wings;
(5)   Was there no Phœbus to denounce the flight
From Heav'n? Nor those ten thousand Eyes of
      Night?
And, were no other eye nor ear of man
Or God awake, yet universal Pan,
    For ever watching at the heart of things,
And Zeus, the Warden of domestic Right,
    And the perennial sanctity of Kings,
Let loose the Fury who, though late
Retarded in the leash of Fate,
    Once loosed, after the Sinner springs;
Over Ocean's heights and hollows,
Into cave and forest follows,

[204]

Into fastest guarded town,
Close on the Sinner's heel insists,
And, turn or baffle as he lists,
  Dogs him inexorably down.

III.

THEREFORE to revenge the debt
  To violated Justice due,
Arméd Hellas hand in hand
  The iron toils of Ares drew
Over water, over land,
Over such a tract of years;   *(6)*
Draught of blood abroad, of tears
  At home, and unexhausted yet:
All the manhood Greece could muster,
  And her hollow ships enclose;
All that Troy from her capacious
  Bosom pouring forth oppose;
By the ships, beneath the wall,
  And about the sandy plain,
Armour-glancing file advancing,
  Fighting, flying, slaying, slain:
And among them, and above them,
Crested Heroes, twain by twain,
  Lance to lance, and thrust to thrust,

Front-erect, and, in a moment,
   One or other roll'd in dust.
Till the better blood of Argos
   Soaking in the Trojan sand,
In her silent half dispeopled
   Cities, more than half unmann'd.
Little more of man to meet
Than the helpless child, or hoary
Spectre of his second childhood,
   Tottering on triple feet,
(7)   Like the idle waifs and strays
Blown together from the ways
   Up and down the windy street.

IV.

But thus it is; All bides the destined Hour
   And Man, albeit with Justice at his side,
Fights in the dark against a secret Power
   Not to be conquer'd—and how pacified?

v.

For, before the Navy flush'd
   Wing from shore, or lifted oar
To foam the purple brush'd;
While about the altar hush'd
   Throng'd the ranks of Greece thick-fold,

[206]

Ancient Chalcas in the bleeding
Volume of the Future reading
  Evil things foresaw, foretold:
That, to revenge some old disgrace
  Befall'n her sylvan train,
Some dumb familiar of the Chase
  By Menelaus slain,
The Goddess Artemis would vex   *(8)*
The fleet of Greece with storms and checks:
  That Troy should not be reach'd at all,
Or—as the Gods themselves divide
In Heav'n to either mortal side—
  If ever reach'd, should never fall—
Unless at such a loss and cost
As counterpoises Won and Lost.

VI.

THE Elder of the Royal Twain
Listen'd in silence, daring not arraign
  Ill omen, or rebuke the raven lips:
Then taking up the tangled skein
  Of Fate, he pointed to the ships;
He sprang aboard: he gave the sign;
  And blazing in his golden arms ahead,
Draws the long Navy in a glittering line
  After him like a meteor o'er the main.

VII.

So from Argos forth: and so
  O'er the rolling waters they,
Till in the roaring To-and-fro
  Of rock-lockt Aulis brought to stay:
(9)   There the Goddess had them fast:
With a bitter northern blast
  Blew ahead and block'd the way:
Day by day delay; to ship
  And tackle damage and decay;
Day by day to Prince and People
  Indignation and dismay.
"All the while that in the ribb'd
"Bosom of their vessels cribb'd,
"Tower-crown'd Troy above the waters
"Yonder, quaffing from the horn
"Of Plenty, laughing them to scorn—"
  So would one to other say;
And man and chief in rage and grief
  Fretted and consumed away.

VIII.

THEN to Sacrifice anew:
  And again within the bleeding
  Volume of the Future reading,

Once again the summon'd Seer

Evil, Evil, still fore-drew.

Day by day, delay, decay *(10)*

To ship and tackle, chief and crew:

And but one way—one only way to appease

The Goddess, and the wind of wrath subdue;

One way of cure so worse than the disease,

As, but to hear propound,

The Atreidæ struck their sceptres to the ground.

IX.

AFTER a death-deep pause,

The Lord of man and armament his voice

Lifted into the silence—"Terrible choice!

" To base imprisonment of wind and flood,

"Whether consign and sacrifice the band

"Of heroes gathered in my name and cause;

"Or thence redeem them by a daughter's blood—

"A daughter's blood shed by a father's hand;

"Shed by a father's hand, and to atone

"The guilt of One—who, could the God endure

"Propitiation by the Life impure,

"Should wash out her transgression with her own."

(11)   X.

BUT, breaking on that iron multitude,
　The Father's cry no kindred echo woke:
And in the sullen silence that ensued
　An unrelenting iron answer spoke.

XI.

AT last his neck to that unnatural yoke
He bow'd: his hand to that unnatural stroke:
With growing purpose, obstinate as the wind
That block'd his fleet, so block'd his better mind,
To all the Father's heart within him blind—
　For thus it fares with men; the seed
　Of Evil, sown by seeming Need,
　　Grows, self-infatuation-nurst,
　From evil Thought to evil Deed,
　　Incomprehensible at first,
　　And to the end of Life accurst.

XII.

AND thus, the blood of that one innocent
Weigh'd light against one great accomplishment,
(12)　　At last—at last—in the meridian blaze
Of Day, with all the Gods in Heaven agaze,
And arméd Greece below—he came to dare—
After due preparation, pomp, and prayer,

He came—the wretched father—came to dare—

   Himself—with sacrificial knife in hand,—

   Before the sacrificial altar stand,

To which—her sweet lips, sweetly wont to sing

   Before him in the banquet-chamber, gagg'd,

Lest one ill word should mar the impious thing;

Her saffron scarf about her fluttering,

   Dumb as an all-but-speaking picture, dragg'd

Through the remorseless soldiery—

                    But soft!—

   While I tell the more than oft-

Told Story, best in silence found,

   Incense-breathing fires aloft

Up into the rising fire,

Into which the stars expire,

   Of Morning mingle; and a sound

As of Rumour at the heel

   Of some great tiding gathers ground;

And from portals that disclose

Before a fragrant air that blows

Them open, what great matter, Sirs,   *(13)*

Thus early Clytemnestra stirs,

Hither through the palace gate

Torch in hand, and step-elate,

Advancing, with the kindled Eyes

As of triumphant Sacrifice?

[211]

[*Enter* CLYTEMNESTRA.

Oh, Clytemnestra, my obeisance
Salutes your coming footstep, as her right
Who rightly occupies the fellow-chair
Of that now ten years widow'd of its Lord.
But—be it at your pleasure ask'd, as answered—
What great occasion, almost ere Night's self
Rekindles into Morning from the Sun,
Has woke your Altar-fire to Sacrifice?

CLYTEMNESTRA.

Oh, never yet did Night—
Night of all Good the Mother, as men say,
Conceive a fairer issue than To-day!
Prepare your ear, Old man, for tidings such
As youthful hope would scarce anticipate.

(14) CHORUS.

I have prepared them for such news as such
Preamble argues.

CLYTEMNESTRA.

What if you be told—
Oh mighty sum in one small figure cast!—
That ten-year-toil'd-for Troy is ours at last?

[212]

CHORUS.

"If told!"—Once more!—the word escaped our ears,
With many a baffled rumour heretofore
Slipp'd down the wind of wasted Expectation.

CLYTEMNESTRA.

Once more then; and with unconditional
Assurance having hit the mark indeed
That Rumour aimed at—Troy, with all the towers
Our burning vengeance leaves aloft, is ours.
Now speak I plainly?

CHORUS.

Oh! to make the tears
That waited to bear witness in the eye
Start, to convict our incredulity!

CLYTEMNESTRA. (15)

Oh, blest conviction that enriches you
That lose the cause with all the victory!

CHORUS.

Ev'n so. But how yourself convinced before?

[213]

CLYTEMNESTRA.

By no less sure a witness than the God.

CHORUS.

What, in a dream?

CLYTEMNESTRA.

I am not apt to trust
The vacillating witnesses of Sleep.

CHORUS.

Ay—but as surely undeluded by
The waking Will, that what we strongly *would*
Imaginates?

CLYTEMNESTRA.

Ay, like a doating girl.

(16)   CHORUS.

Oh, Clytemnestra, pardon mere Old Age
That, after so long starving upon Hope,
But slowly brooks his own Accomplishment.
The Ten-year war is done then! Troy is taken!
The Gods have told you, and the Gods tell true—
But—how? and when?

[214]

CLYTEMNESTRA.

Ev'n with the very birth
Of the good Night which mothers this best Day.

CHORUS.

To-day! To-night! but of Night's work in Troy
Who should inform the scarce awaken'd ear
Of Morn in Argos?

CLYTEMNESTRA.

       Hephaistos, the lame God,
And spriteliest of mortal messengers;
Who, springing from the bed of burning Troy,
Hither, by fore-devis'd Intelligence
Agreed upon between my Lord and me,
Posted from dedicated Height to Height
The reach of land and sea that lies between.   *(9)*
And, first to catch him and begin the game,
Did Ida fire her forest-pine, and, waving
Handed him on to that Hermæan steep
Of Lemnos; Lemnos to the summit of
Zeus-consecrated Athos lifted; whence,
As by the giant taken, so despatch'd,
The Torch of Conquest, traversing the wide
Ægæan with a sunbeam-stretching stride,

Struck up the drowsy watchers on Makistos;
Who, flashing back the challenge, flash'd it on
To those who watch'd on the Messapian height.
With whose quick-kindling heather heap'd and fired
The meteor-bearded messenger refresh'd,
Clearing Asopus at a bound, struck fire
From old Kithæron; and, so little tired
As waxing even wanton with the sport,
Over the sleeping water of Gorgopis
Sprung to the Rock of Corinth; thence to the cliffs
Which stare down the Saronic Gulf, that now
Began to shiver in the creeping Dawn;
Whence, for a moment on the neighbouring top
Of Arachnæum lighting, one last bound
Brought him to Agamemnon's battlements.
(10) By such gigantic strides in such a Race
Where First and Last alike are Conquerors,
Posted the travelling Fire, whose Father-light
Ida conceived of burning Troy to-night.

CHORUS.

Woman, your words man-metal ring, and strike
Ev'n from the tuneless fibre of Old Age
Such martial unison as from the lips
Shall break into full Pæan by and by.

CLYTEMNESTRA.

Aye, think—think—think, old man, and in your soul,
As if 'twere mirror'd in your outward eye,
Imagine what wild work a-doing there—
In Troy—to-night—to-day—this moment—how
Harmoniously, as in one vessel meet
Esil and Oil, meet Triumph and Despair,
Sluiced by the sword along the reeking street,
On which the Gods look down from burning air.
Slain, slaying—dying, dead—about the dead
Fighting to die themselves—maidens and wives
Lockt by the locks, with their barbarian young,   *(11)*
And torn away to slavery and shame
By hands all reeking with their Champion's blood.
Until, with execution weary, we
Fling down our slaughter-satiated swords,
To gorge ourselves on the unfinish'd feasts
Of poor old Priam and his sons; and then,
Roll'd on rich couches never spread for us,
Ev'n now our sleep-besotted foreheads turn
Up to the very Sun that rises here.
Such is the lawful game of those who win
Upon so just a quarrel—so long fought:
Provided always that, with jealous care,
Retaliation wreaking upon those

[217   ]

Who our insulted Gods upon them drew,

We push not Riot to *their* Altar-foot;

Remembering, on whichever mortal side

Engaged, the Gods are Gods in heav'n and earth,

And not to be insulted unavenged.

This let us take to heart, and keep in sight;

Lest, having run victoriously thus far,

And turn'd the very pillar of our race,

Before we reach the long'd-for goal of Home

Nemesis overtake, or trip us up;

(12) Some ere safe shipp'd: or, launch'd upon the foam,

Ere touch'd the threshold of their native shore;

Yea, or that reach'd, the threshold of the door

Of their own home; from whatsoever corner

The jealous Power is ever on the watch

To compass arrogant Prosperity.

These are a woman's words; for men to take,

Or disregarded drop them, as they will;

Enough for me, if having won the stake,

I pray the Gods with us to keep it still.

[*Exit* CLYTEMNESTRA.

CHORUS.

OH, sacred Night,

From whose unfathomable breast

Creative Order formed and saw

Chaos emerging into Law:
And now, committed with Eternal Right,
Who didst with star-entangled net invest
　So close the guilty City as she slept,
That when the deadly fisher came to draw,
Not one of all the guilty fry through crept.

II.　　　　　　　　　　　　　(13)

　Oh, Nemesis,
Night's daughter! in whose bosoming abyss
　Secretly sitting by the Sinner's sleeve,
　Thou didst with self-confusion counterweave
His plot; and when the fool his arrow sped,
　Thine after-shot didst only not dismiss
Till certain not to miss the guilty head.

III.

Some think the Godhead, couching at his ease
Deep in the purple Heav'ns, serenely sees
　Insult the altar of Eternal Right.
　Fools!　For though Fortune seem to misrequite,
　And Retribution for awhile forget;
　Sooner or later she reclaims the debt
With usury that triples the amount
Of Nemesis with running Time's account.

IV.

FOR soon or late sardonic Fate
   With Man against himself conspires;
   Puts on the mask of his desires:
Up the steps of Time elate
Leads him blinded with his pride,
And gathering as he goes along
The fuel of his suicide:
Until having topp'd the pyre
Which Destiny permits no higher,
Ambition sets himself on fire;
In conflagration like the crime
Conspicuous through the world and time
Down amidst his brazen walls
The accumulated Idol falls
To shapeless ashes; Demigod
Under the vulgar hoof down-trod
Whose neck he trod on; not an eye
To weep his fall, nor lip to sigh
For him a prayer; or, if there were,
No God to listen, or reply.

V.

AND as the son his father's guilt may rue;
   And, by retort of justice, what the son

(14)

Has sinn'd, to ruin on the father run;
So may the many help to pay the due
  Of guilt, remotely implicate with one.
And as the tree 'neath which a felon cowers,　　(15)
  With all its branch is blasted by the bolt
  Of Justice launch'd from Heav'n at *his* revolt;
Thus with old Priam, with his royal line,
  Kindred and people; yea, the very towers
They crouch'd in, built by masonry divine.

VI.

LIKE a dream through sleep she glided
  Through the silent city gate,
By a guilty Hermes guided
On the feather'd feet of Theft;
Leaving between those she left
And those she fled to lighted Discord,
  Unextinguishable Hate;
Leaving him whom least she should,
Menelaus brave and good,
Scarce believing in the mutter'd
Rumour, in the worse than utter'd
  Omen of the wailing maidens,
Of the shaken hoary head;
Of deserted board and bed.

For the phantom of the lost one
Haunts him in the wonted places;
(16)   Hall and Chamber, where he paces
Hither, Thither, listening, looking,
   Phantom-like himself alone;
Till he comes to loathe the faces
Of the marble mute Colossi,
   Godlike forms, and half-divine,
   Founders of the Royal line,
   Who with all unfalter'd Quiet
   Witness all and make no sign.
But the silence of the chambers,
   And the shaken hoary head,
And the voices of the mourning
Women, and of ocean wailing,
Over which with unavailing
Arms he reaches, as to hail
The phantom of a flying sail—
   All but answer, Fled! fled! fled!
   False! dishonour'd! worse than dead!

VII.

At last the sun goes down along the bay,
And with him drags detested Day.
He sleeps; and, dream-like as she fled, beside
His pillow, Dream indeed, behold! his Bride

Once more in more than bridal beauty stands; *(17)*
But, ever as he reaches forth his hands,
Slips from them back into the viewless deep,
On those soft silent wings that walk the ways of sleep.

VIII.

Not beside thee in the chamber,
    Menelaus, any more;
But with him she fled with, pillow'd
On the summer softly-billow'd
Ocean, into dimple wreathing
    Underneath a breeze of amber
Air that, as from Eros breathing,
    Fill'd the sail and flew before;
Floating on the summer seas
Like some sweet Effigies
Of Eirene's self, or sweeter
    Aphrodite, sweeter still:
With the Shepherd, from whose luckless
    Hand upon the Phrygian hill
Of the three Immortals, She
The fatal prize of Beauty bore, *(18)*
Floating with him o'er the foam
She rose from, to the Shepherd's home
    On the Ionian shore.

[223]

IX.

Down from the City to the water-side
Old Priam, with his princely retinue,
By many a wondering Phrygian follow'd, drew
To welcome and bear in the Goddess-bride,
Whom some propitious wind of Fortune blew
From whence they knew not o'er the waters wide,
Among the Trojan people to abide,
A pledge of Love and Joy for ever—Yes;
As one who drawing from the leopardess
Her suckling cub, and, fascinated by
The little Savage of the lustrous eye,
Bears home, for all to fondle and caress,
And be the very darling of the house
It makes a den of blood of by and by.

X.

For the wind, that amber blew,
Tempest in its bosom drew,
(19)   Soon began to hiss and roar;
And the sweet Effigies
That amber breeze and summer seas
Had wafted to the Ionian shore,
By swift metamorphosis

[224]

Turn'd into some hideous, hated,
Fury of Revenge, and fated
  Hierophant of Nemesis;
Who, growing with the day and hour,
Grasp'd the wall, and topp'd the tower,
And, when the time came, by its throat
The victim City seized, and smote.

XI.

BUT now to be resolved, whether indeed
  Those fires of Night spoke truly, or mistold
  To cheat a doating woman; for, behold,
Advancing from the shore with solemn speed,
  A Herald from the Fleet, his footsteps roll'd
In dust, Haste's thirsty consort, but his brow
Check-shadow'd with the nodding Olive-bough;
Who shall interpret us the speechless sign
Of the fork'd tongue that preys upon the pine.

HERALD. *(20)*

Oh, Fatherland of Argos, back to whom
After ten years do I indeed return
Under the dawn of this auspicious day!
Of all the parted anchors of lost Hope

That this, depended least on, yet should hold;

Amid so many men to me so dear

About me dying, that myself exempt

Return to live what yet of life remains

Among my own; among my own at last

To share the blest communion of the Dead!

Oh, welcome, welcome, welcome once again

My own dear Country and the light she draws

From the benignant Heav'ns; and all the Gods

Who guard her; Zeus Protector first of all;

And Phœbus, by this all-restoring dawn

Who heals the wounds his arrows dealt so fast

Beside Scamander; and not last nor least

Among the Powers engaged upon our side,

Hermes, the Herald's Patron, and his Pride;

Who, having brought me safely through the war,

Now brings me back to tell the victory

Into my own belovéd country's ear;

(21) Who, all the more by us, the more away,

Beloved, will greet with Welcome no less dear

This remnant of the unremorseful spear.

And, oh, you Temples, Palaces, and throned

Colossi, that affront the rising sun,

If ever yet, your marble foreheads now

Bathe in the splendour of returning Day

To welcome back your so long absent Lord;

Who by Zeus' self directed to the spot
Of Vengeance, and the special instrument
Of Retribution put into his hands,
Has undermined, uprooted, and destroy'd,
Till scarce one stone upon another stands,
The famous Citadel, that, deeply cast
For crime, has all the forfeit paid at last.

CHORUS.

Oh hail and welcome, Herald of good news!
Welcome and hail! and doubt not thy return
As dear to us as thee.

HERALD.

To me so dear,
After so long despair'd of, that, for fear
Life's after-draught the present should belie,   *(22)*
One might implore the Gods ev'n now to die!

CHORUS.

Oh, your soul hunger'd after home!

HERALD.
                                        So sore,
That sudden satisfaction of once more
Return weeps out its surfeit at my eyes.

CHORUS.

And ours, you see, contagiously, no less
The same long grief, and sudden joy, confess.

HERALD.

What! Argos for her missing children yearn'd
As they for her, then?

CHORUS.

Ay; perhaps and more,
Already pining with an inward sore.

(23)   HERALD.
How so?

CHORUS.

Nay, Silence, that has best endured
The pain, may best dismiss the memory.

HERALD.

Ev'n so. For who, unless the God himself,
Expects to live his life without a flaw?
Why, once begin to open that account,
Might not *we* tell for ten good years to come
Of all we suffer'd in the ten gone by?

[228]

Not the mere course and casualty of war,

Alarum, March, Battle, and such hard knocks

As foe with foe expects to give and take;

But all the complement of miseries

That go to swell a long campaign's account.

Cramm'd close aboard the ships, hard bed, hard board:

Or worse perhaps while foraging ashore

In winter time; when if not from the walls,

Pelted from Heav'n by Day, to couch by Night

Between the falling dews and rising damps   (24)

That elf'd the locks, and set the body fast

With cramp and ague; or, to mend the matter,

Good mother Ida from her winter top

Flinging us down a coverlet of snow.

Or worst perhaps in Summer, toiling in

The bloody harvest-field of torrid sand,

When not an air stirr'd the fierce Asian noon,

And ev'n the sea sleep-sicken'd in his bed.

But why lament the Past, as past it is?

If idle for the Dead who feel no more,

Idler for us to whom this blissful Dawn

Shines doubly bright against the stormy Past;

Who, after such predicament and toil,

Boast, once more standing on our mother soil,

   That Zeus, who sent us to revenge the crime

Upon the guilty people, now recalls

AGAMEMNON.

To hang their trophies on our temple walls
　For monumental heir-looms to all time.

CHORUS.

　Oh, but Old age, however slow to learn,
　Not slow to learn, nor after you repeat,
(25) Lesson so welcome, Herald of the Fleet!
　But here is Clytemnestra; be you first
　To bless her ears, as mine, with news so sweet.

CLYTEMNESTRA.

I sang my Song of Triumph ere he came,
Alone I sang it while the City slept,
And these wise Senators, with winking eyes,
Look'd grave, and weigh'd mistrustfully my word,
As the light coinage of a woman's brain.
And so they went their way.　But not the less
From those false fires I lit my altar up,
And, woman-wise, held on my song, until
The City taking up the note from me,
Scarce knowing why, about that altar flock'd,
Where, like the Priest of Victory, I stood,
Torch-handed, drenching in triumphant wine
The flame that from the smouldering incense rose.
Now what more needs?　This Herald of the Day

Adds but another witness to the Night;

And I will hear no more from other lips,

Till from my husband Agamemnon all,

Whom with all honour I prepare to meet. *(26)*

Oh, to a loyal woman what so sweet

As once more wide the gate of welcome fling

To the loved Husband whom the Gods once more

After long travail home triumphant bring;

Where he shall find her, as he left before,

Fix'd like a trusty watchdog at the door,

Tractable him-ward, but inveterate

Against the doubtful stranger at the gate;

And not a seal within the house but still

Inviolate, under a woman's trust

Incapable of taint as gold of rust.

[*Exit* CLYTEMNESTRA.

HERALD.

A boast not misbeseeming a true woman.

CHORUS.

For then no boast at all. But she says well;

And Time interprets all. Enough for us

To praise the Gods for Agamemnon's safe,

And more than safe return. And Menelaus,

The other half of Argos—What of him?

HERALD.

(27) Those that I most would gladden with good news,
And on a day like this—with fair but false
I dare not.

CHORUS.

What, must fair then needs be false?

HERALD.

Old man, the Gods grant somewhat, and withhold
As seems them good: a time there is for Praise,
A time for Supplication: nor is it well
To twit the celebration of their largess,
Reminding them of something they withhold.

CHORUS.

Yet till we know how much withheld or granted,
We know not how the balance to adjust
Of Supplication or of Praise.

HERALD.
Alas,
The Herald who returns with downcast eyes,
(28) And leafless brow prophetic of Reverse,
Let him at once—at once let him, I say,
Lay the whole burden of Ill-tidings down

In the mid market-place.   But why should one
Returning with the garland on his brow
Be stopp'd to name the single missing leaf
Of which the Gods have stinted us!

CHORUS.
Alas,
The putting of a fearful question by
Is but to ill conjecture worse reply!
You bring not back then—do not leave behind—
What Menelaus was?

HERALD.
The Gods forbid!
Safe shipp'd with all the host.

CHORUS.
Well but—how then?
Surely no tempest—

HERALD.   (29)
Ay! by that one word
Hitting the centre of a boundless sorrow!

CHORUS.
Well, but if peradventure from the fleet
Parted—not lost?

AGAMEMNON.

HERALD.

None but the eye of Day,
Now woke, knows all the havoc of the Night.
For Night it was; all safe aboard—sail set,
And oars all beating home; when suddenly,
As if those old antagonists had sworn
New strife between themselves for our destruction,
The sea, that tamely let us mount his back,
Began to roar and plunge under a lash
Of tempest from the thundering heavens so fierce
As, falling on our fluttering navy, some
Scatter'd, or whirl'd away like flakes of foam;
Or, huddling wave on wave, so ship on ship
Like fighting eagles on each other fell,
(30) And beak, and wing, and claws, entangled, tore
To pieces one another, or dragg'd down.
So when at last the tardy-rising Sun
Survey'd, and show'd, the havoc Night had done,
We, whom some God—or Fortune's self, I think—
Seizing the helm, had steer'd as man could not,
Beheld the waste Ægæan wilderness
Strown with the shatter'd forest of the fleet,
Trunk, branch, and foliage; and yet worse, I ween,
The flower of Argos floating dead between.
Then we, scarce trusting in our own escape,

[234]

And saving such as yet had life to save,

Along the heaving wilderness of wave

Went ruminating, who of those we miss'd

Might yet survive, who lost; the saved, no doubt,

As sadly speculating after us.

Of whom, if Menelaus—and the Sun,

(A prayer which all the Gods in Heav'n fulfil!)

Behold him on the water breathing still;

Doubt not that Zeus, under whose special showers

And suns the royal growth of Atreus towers,

Will not let perish stem, and branch, and fruit,

By loss of one corroborating root.

CHORUS.   (31)

OH, Helen, Helen, Helen! oh, fair name

And fatal, of the fatal-fairest dame

   That ever blest or blinded human eyes!

Of mortal women Queen beyond compare,

   As she whom the foam lifted to the skies

Is Queen of all who breathe immortal air!

   Whoever, and from whatsoever wells

   Of Divination, drew the syllables

By which we name thee; who shall ever dare

In after time the fatal name to wear,

Or would, to be so fatal, be so fair!

Whose dowry was a Husband's shame;
Whose nuptial torch was Troy in flame;
Whose bridal Chorus, groans and cries;
Whose banquet, brave men's obsequies;
Whose Hymenæal retinue,
The winged dogs of War that flew
Over lands and over seas,
Following the tainted breeze,
Till, Scamander reed among,
Their fiery breath and bloody tongue
The fatal quarry found and slew;
(32) And, having done the work to which
The God himself halloo'd them, back
Return a maim'd and scatter'd pack.

II.

And he for whose especial cause
  Zeus his winged instrument
With the lightning in his claws
  From the throne of thunder sent:
He for whom the sword was drawn:
Mountain ashes fell'd and sawn;
  And the armed host of Hellas
Cramm'd within them, to discharge
On the shore to bleed at large;

[236   ]

He, in mid accomplishment
Of Justice, from his glory rent!
What ten years had hardly won,
In a single night undone;
And on earth what saved and gain'd,
By the ravin sea distrain'd.

III.

SUCH is the sorrow of this royal house;
   But none in all the City but forlorn
Under its own peculiar sorrow bows. *(33)*
For the stern God who, deaf to human love,
   Grudges the least abridgment of the tale
Of human blood once pledged to him, above
The centre of the murder-dealing crowd
   Suspends in air his sanguinary scale;
And for the blooming Hero gone a-field
   Homeward remits a beggarly return
Of empty helmet, fallen sword and shield,
   And some light ashes in a little urn.

IV.

THEN wild and high goes up the cry
To heav'n, "So true! so brave! so fair!
"The young colt of the flowing hair

"And flaming eye, and now—look there!

"Ashes and arms!" or, "Left behind

"Unburied, in the sun and wind

"To wither, or become the feast

"Of bird obscene, or unclean beast;

"The good, the brave, without a grave—

"All to redeem *her* from the shame

"To which she sold her self and name!"—

(34) For such insinuation in the dark

About the City travels like a spark;

 Till the pent tempest into lightning breaks,

And takes the topmost pinnacle for mark.

v.

BUT avaunt all evil omen!

 Perish many, so the State

 They die for live inviolate;

Which, were all her mortal leafage

 In the blast of Ares scatter'd,

 So herself at heart unshatter'd,

In due season she retrieves

All her wasted wealth of leaves,

And age on age shall spread and rise

To cover earth and breathe the skies.

While the rival at her side

Who the wrath of Heav'n defied,

By the lashing blast, or flashing

Bolt of Heav'n comes thunder-crashing,

Top and lop, and trunk and bough,

Down, for ever down.   And now,

He to whom the Zeus of Vengeance

  Did commit the bolt of Fate—   (35)

Agamemnon—how shall I,

With a Pæan not too high

For mortal glory, to provoke

From the Gods a counter-stroke;

Nor below desert so lofty

  Suitably felicitate?

Such as chasten'd Age for due

May give, and Manhood take for true.

For, as many men comply

From founts no deeper than the eye

  With others' sorrows; many more,

With a Welcome from the lips,

That far the halting heart outstrips,

  Fortune's Idol fall before.

Son of Atreus, I premise,

  When at first the means and manhood

Of the cities thou didst stake

For a wanton woman's sake,

  I might grudge the sacrifice;

But, the warfare once begun,
Hardly fought and hardly won,
Now from Glory's overflowing
Horn of Welcome all her glowing
(36)   Honours, and with uninvidious
Hand, before your advent throwing,
I salute, and bid thee welcome,
Son of Atreus, Agamemnon,
Zeus' revenging Right-hand, Lord
    Of taken Troy and righted Greece:
Bid thee from the roving throne
    Of War the reeking steed release;
Leave the laurell'd ship to ride
Anchor'd in her country's side,
And resume the royal helm
Of thy long-abandon'd realm:
What about the State or Throne
Of good or evil since has grown,
    Alter, cancel, or complete;
And to well or evil-doer,
    Even-handed Justice mete.

Enter A<small>GAMEMNON</small> *in his chariot,* C<small>ASSANDRA</small>   (37)
following in another.

A<small>GAMEMNON</small>.

First, as first due, my Country I salute,

And all her tutelary Gods; all those

Who, having sent me forth, now bring me back,

After full retribution wrought on those

Who retribution owed us, and the Gods

In full consistory determined; each,

With scarce a swerving eye to Mercy's side,

Dropping his vote into the urn of blood.

Caught and consuming in whose fiery wrath,

The stately City, from her panting ashes

Into the nostril of revolted Heav'n*

Gusts of expiring opulence puffs up.[1]

For which, I say, the Gods alone be thank'd;

By whose connivance round about the wall

We drew the belt of Ares, and laid bare

The flank of Ilium to the Lion-horse,[2]   (38)

---

* " Into the face of the revolted heavens." (Edition of 1876.)

[1] *Those who know the Greek will scarce accuse me of over-alliteration in this line, which runs in the original thus,*

     Spodos propempei pionas ploutou pnoas.

[2] *Dr. Donaldson tells us in his Varronianus (says Paley), that the Lion was the symbol of the Atreidæ; and Pausanias writes that part of the ancient walls of Mycenæ was yet standing in his day, and Lions on the gate. Wordsworth (Athens and Attica) says the Lion was often set up to commemorate a victory.*

Who sprung by night over the city wall,

And foal'd his iron progeny within,

About the setting of the Pleiades.[1]

Thus much by way of prelude to the Gods.

For you, oh white-hair'd senators of Argos,

Your measured Welcome, I receive for just;

Aware on what a tickle base of fortune

The monument of human Glory stands;

And, for humane congratulation, knowing

How, smile as may the mask, the man behind

Frets at the fortune that degrades his own.

This, having heard of from the wise, myself,

From long experience in the ways of men,

Can vouch for—what a shadow of a shade

Is human loyalty; and, as a proof,

Of all the Host that fill'd the Grecian ship,

(39) And pour'd at large along the field of Troy,

One only Chief—and he, too, like yourself,

At first with little stomach for the cause—

The wise Odysseus—once in harness, he

With all his might pull'd in the yoke with me,

Through envy, obloquy, and opposition:

And in Odysseus' honour, live or dead—

For yet we know not which—shall this be said.

Of which enough. For other things of moment

[1] *"About the setting of the Pleiades," is about the end of Autumn.*

[242]

To which you point, or human or divine,

We shall forthwith consider and adjudge

In seasonable council; what is well,

Or in our absence well deserving, well

Establish and requite; what not, redress

With salutary caution; or, if need,

With the sharp edge of Justice; and to health

Restore, and right, our ailing Commonwealth.

Now, first of all, by my own altar-hearth

To thank the Gods for my return, and pray

That Victory, which thus far by my side

Has flown with us, with us may still abide.

Enter CLYTEMNESTRA *from the Palace.* *(40)*

CLYTEMNESTRA.

Oh Men of Argos, count it not a shame

If a fond wife, and one whom riper years

From Youth's becoming bashfulness excuse,

Dares own her love before the face of men;

Nor leaving it for others to enhance,

Simply declares the wretched widowhood

Which these ten years she has endured, since first

Her husband Agamemnon went to Troy.

'Tis no light matter, let me tell you, Sirs,

A woman left in charge of house and home—

[243]

And when that house and home a Kingdom—and
She left alone to rule it—and ten years!
Beside dissent and discontent at home,
Storm'd from abroad with contrary reports,
Now fair, now foul; but still as time wore on
Growing more desperate; as dangerous
Unto the widow'd kingdom as herself.
Why, had my husband there but half the wounds
Fame stabb'd him with, he were before me now,
Not the whole man we see him, but a body
Gash'd into network; ay, or, had he died

(41) But half as often as Report gave out,
He would have needed thrice the cloak of earth
To cover him, that triple Geryon
Lies buried under in the world below.
Thus, back and forward baffled, and at last
So desperate—that, if I be here alive
To tell the tale, no thanks to me for that,
Whose hands had twisted round my neck the noose
Which others loosen'd—my Orestes too
In whose expanding manhood day by day
My Husband I perused—and, by the way,
Whom wonder not, my Lord, not seeing here;
My simple mother-love, and jealousy
Of civil treason—ever as you know,
Most apt to kindle when the lord away—

[244]

Having bestow'd him, out of danger's reach,

With Strophius of Phocis, wholly yours

Bound by the generous usages of war,

That make the once-won foe so fast a friend.

Thus, widow'd of my son as of his sire,

No wonder if I wept—not drops, but showers,

The ten years' night through which I watch'd in vain

The star that was to bring him back to me;   (42)

Or, if I slept, a sleep so thin as scared

Even at the slight incursion of the gnat;

And yet more thick with visionary terrors

Than thrice the waking while had occupied.

Well, I have borne all this: all this have borne,

Without a grudge against the wanderer,

Whose now return makes more than rich amends

For all ungrateful absence—Agamemnon,

My Lord and Husband; Lord of Argos; Troy's

Confounder; Mainstay of the realm of Greece;

And Master-column of the house of Atreus—

Oh wonder not that I accumulate

All honour and endearment on his head!

If to his country, how much more to me,

Welcome, as land to sailors long at sea,

Or water in the desert; whose return

Is fire to the forsaken winter-hearth;

Whose presence, like the rooted Household Tree

That, winter-dead so long, anew puts forth
To shield us from the Dogstar, what time Zeus
Wrings the tart vintage into blissful juice.
Down from the chariot thou standest in,
Crown'd with the flaming towers of Troy, descend,
(43) And to this palace, rich indeed with thee,
But beggar-poor without, return! And ye,
My women, carpet all the way before,
From the triumphal carriage to the door,
With all the gold and purple in the chest
   Stored these ten years; and to what purpose stored,
   Unless to strew the footsteps of their Lord
Returning to his unexpected rest!

AGAMEMNON.

Daughter of Leda, Mistress of my house,
Beware lest loving Welcome of your Lord,
Measuring itself by his protracted absence,
Exceed the bound of rightful compliment,
And better left to other lips than yours.
Address me not, address me not, I say
With dust-adoring adulation, meeter
For some barbarian Despot from his slave;
Nor with invidious Purple strew my way,
Fit only for the footstep of a God
Lighting from Heav'n to earth. Let whoso will

Trample their glories underfoot, not I.

Woman, I charge you, honour me no more

Than as the man I am; if honour-worth,

Needing no other trapping but the fame (44)

Of the good deed I clothe myself withal;

And knowing that, of all their gifts to man,

No greater gift than Self-sobriety

The Gods vouchsafe him in the race of life:

Which, after thus far running, if I reach

The goal in peace, it shall be well for me.

CLYTEMNESTRA.

Why, how think you old Priam would have walk'd

Had he return'd to Troy your conqueror,

As you to Hellas his?

AGAMEMNON.

What then? Perhaps

Voluptuary Asiatic-like,

On gold and purple.

CLYTEMNESTRA.

Well, and grudging this,

When all that out before your footsteps flows

Ebbs back into the treasury again;

[247]

Think how much more, had Fate the tables turn'd,
(45) Irrevocably from those coffers gone,
For those barbarian feet to walk upon,
To buy your ransom back?

AGAMEMNON.

Enough, enough!
I know my reason.

CLYTEMNESTRA.

What! the jealous God?
Or, peradventure, yet more envious man?

AGAMEMNON.

And *that* of no small moment.

CLYTEMNESTRA.

No; the one
Sure proof of having won what others would.

AGAMEMNON.

No matter—Strife but ill becomes a woman.

CLYTEMNESTRA.

And frank submission to her simple wish
How well becomes the Soldier in his strength!

[248]

AGAMEMNON.   *(46)*

And I must then submit?

CLYTEMNESTRA.

Aye, Agamemnon,
Deny me not this first Desire on this
First Morning of your long-desired Return.

AGAMEMNON.

But not till I have put these sandals off,
That, slave-like, too officiously would pander
Between the purple and my dainty feet.
For fear, for fear indeed, some Jealous eye
From heav'n above, or earth below, should strike
The Man who walks the earth Immortal-like.
So much for that.   For this same royal maid,
Cassandra, daughter of King Priamus,
Whom, as the flower of all the spoil of Troy,
The host of Hellas dedicates to me;
Entreat her gently; knowing well that none
But submit hardly to a foreign yoke;
And those of Royal blood most hardly brook.
That if I sin thus trampling underfoot

[249   ]

A woof in which the Heav'ns themselves are dyed,

(47) The jealous God may less resent his crime,

Who mingles human mercy with his pride.

CLYTEMNESTRA.

The Sea there is, and shall the sea be dried?

Fount inexhaustibler of purple grain

Than all the wardrobes of the world could drain;

And Earth there is, whose dusky closets hide

The precious metal wherewith not in vain

The Gods themselves this Royal house provide;

For what occasion worthier, or more meet,

Than now to carpet the victorious feet

Of Him who, thus far having done their will,

Shall now their last About-to-be fulfil.

[AGAMEMNON *descends from his chariot, and goes with*
CLYTEMNESTRA *into the house,* CASSANDRA *remaining.*]

CHORUS.

ABOUT the nations runs a saw,

That Over-good ill-fortune breeds;

And true that, by the mortal law,

(48)   Fortune her spoilt children feeds

To surfeit, such as sows the seeds

Of Insolence, that, as it grows,

The flower of Self-repentance blows.

And true that Virtue often leaves
The marble walls and roofs of kings,
And underneath the poor man's eaves
On smoky rafter folds her wings.

II.

THUS the famous city, flown
With insolence, and overgrown,
Is humbled: all her splendour blown
To smoke: her glory laid in dust;
Who shall say by doom unjust?
But should He to whom the wrong
Was done, and Zeus himself made strong
To do the vengeance He decreed—
At last returning with the meed
　　He wrought for—should the jealous Eye
　　That blights full-blown prosperity
Pursue him—then indeed, indeed,
Man should hoot and scare aloof　　　　　　(49)
Good-fortune lighting on the roof;
Yea, even Virtue's self forsake
If Glory follow'd in the wake;
Seeing bravest, best, and wisest
　　But the playthings of a day,
Which a shadow can trip over,
　　And a breath can puff away.

[251]

CLYTEMNESTRA (*re-entering*).

Yet for a moment let me look on her—
This, then, is Priam's daughter—
Cassandra, and a Prophetess, whom Zeus
Has giv'n into my hands to minister
Among my slaves. Didst thou prophesy that?
Well—some more famous have so fall'n before—
Ev'n Herakles, the son of Zeus, they say
Was sold, and bow'd his shoulder to the yoke.

CHORUS.

And, if needs must a captive, better far
Of some old house that affluent Time himself
(50) Has taught the measure of prosperity,
Than drunk with sudden superfluity.

CLYTEMNESTRA.

Ev'n so. You hear? Therefore at once descend
From that triumphal chariot—And yet
She keeps her station still, her laurel on,
Disdaining to make answer.

CHORUS.

　　　　　　　　Nay, perhaps,
Like some stray swallow blown across the seas,
Interpreting no twitter but her own.

[　252　]

CLYTEMNESTRA.

But, if barbarian, still interpreting
The universal language of the hand.

CHORUS.

Which yet again she does not seem to see,
Staring before her with wide-open eyes
As in a trance.

CLYTEMNESTRA. (51)

Ay, ay, a prophetess—
Phœbus Apollo's minion once—Whose now?
A time will come for her. See you to it:
A greater business now is on my hands:
For lo! the fire of Sacrifice is lit,
And the grand victim by the altar stands.

[*Exit* CLYTEMNESTRA.

CHORUS (*continuing*).

Still a mutter'd and half-blind
Superstition haunts mankind,
That, by some divine decree
Yet by mortal undivined
Mortal Fortune must not over-
Leap the bound he cannot see;

[253]

For that even wisest labour
   Lofty-building, builds to fall,
Evermore a jealous neighbour
   Undermining floor and wall.
So that on the smoothest water
   Sailing, in a cloudless sky,
The wary merchant overboard
Flings something of his precious hoard
   To pacify the jealous eye,
That will not suffer man to swell
Over human measure. Well,
As the Gods have order'd we
Must take—I know not—let it be.
But, by rule of retribution,
   Hidden, too, from human eyes,
Fortune in her revolution,
   If she fall, shall fall to rise;
And the hand of Zeus dispenses
   Even measure in the main:
One short harvest recompenses
   With a glut of golden grain;
So but men in patience wait
   Fortune's counter-revolution
Axled on eternal Fate;
And the Sisters three that twine,

(52)

Cut not short the vital line;
For indeed the purple seed
Of life once shed—

CASSANDRA.

Phœbus Apollo!

CHORUS. (53)

          Hark!
The lips at last unlocking.

CASSANDRA.

      Phœbus! Phœbus!

CHORUS.

Well, what of Phœbus, maiden? though a name
'Tis but disparagement to call upon
In misery.

CASSANDRA.

Apollo! Apollo! Again!
Oh, the burning arrow through the brain!
    Phœbus Apollo! Apollo!

CHORUS.

       Seemingly
Possess'd indeed—whether by—

CASSANDRA.

Phœbus! Phœbus!
Thorough trampled ashes, blood, and fiery rain,
(54) Over water seething, and behind the breathing
Warhorse in the darkness—till you rose again—
Took the helm—took the rein—

CHORUS.

As one that half asleep at dawn recalls
A night of Horror!

CASSANDRA.

Hither, whither, Phœbus? And with whom,
Leading me, lighting me—

CHORUS.

I can answer that—

CASSANDRA.

Down to what slaughter-house?
Foh! the smell of carnage through the door
Scares me from it—drags me tow'rd it—
Phœbus! Apollo! Apollo!

[256]

CHORUS.   (55)

One of the dismal prophet-pack, it seems,
That hunt the trail of blood.   But here at fault—
This is no den of slaughter, but the house
Of Agamemnon.

CASSANDRA.

Down upon the towers
Phantoms of two mangled Children hover—and a fam-
      ish'd man,
At an empty table glaring, seizes and devours!

CHORUS.

Thyestes and his children!   Strange enough
For any maiden from abroad to know,
Or, knowing—

CASSANDRA.

And look! in the chamber below
The terrible Woman, listening, watching,
Under a mask, preparing the blow
In the fold of her robe—

CHORUS.   (56)

Nay, but again at fault:
For in the tragic story of this House—

AGAMEMNON.

Unless, indeed, the fatal Helen—

No woman—

CASSANDRA.

No Woman—Tisiphone! Daughter

Of Tartarus—love-grinning Woman above,

Dragon-tail'd under—honey-tongued, Harpy-claw'd,

Into the glittering meshes of slaughter

She wheedles, entices, him into the poisonous

Fold of the serpent—

CHORUS.

Peace, mad woman, peace!

Whose stony lips once open vomit out

Such uncouth horrors.

CASSANDRA.

I tell you the lioness

Slaughters the Lion asleep; and lifting

(57) Her blood-dripping fangs buried deep in his mane,

Glaring about her insatiable, bellowing

Bounds hither—Phœbus, Apollo, Apollo, Apollo!

Whither have you led me, under night alive with fire,

Through the trampled ashes of the city of my sire,

From my slaughtered kinsmen, fallen throne, insulted
shrine,

Slave-like to be butcher'd, led the daughter of a Royal
line!

[258]

Chorus.

And so returning, like a nightingale
Returning to the passionate note of woe
By which the silence first was broken!

Cassandra.

Oh,

A nightingale, a nightingale, indeed,
That, as she "Itys! Itys! Itys!" so
I "Helen! Helen! Helen!" having sung
Amid my people, now to those who flung
And trampled on the nest, and slew the young,
Keep crying "Blood! blood! blood!" and none will heed! *(58)*
Now what for me is this prophetic weed,
And what for me is this immortal crown,
Who like a wild swan from Scamander's reed
Chaunting her death-song float Cocytus-down?
There let the fatal Leaves to perish lie!
To perish, or enrich some other brow
With that all-fatal gift of Prophecy
They palpitated under Him who now,
Checking his flaming chariot in mid sky,
With divine irony sees disadorn
The wretch his love has made the people's scorn,
The raving quean, the mountebank, the scold,
Who, wrapt up in the ruin she foretold

With those who would not listen, now descends
To that dark kingdom where his empire ends.

CHORUS.

Strange that Apollo should the laurel wreath
Of Prophecy he crown'd your head withal
Himself disgrace.   But something have we heard
Of some divine revenge for slighted love.

(59)   ### CASSANDRA.

Ay—and as if in malice to attest
    With one expiring beam of Second-sight
Wherewith his victim he has cursed and blest,
    Ere quench'd for ever in descending night;
As from behind a veil no longer peeps
The Bride of Truth, nor from their hidden deeps
Darkle the waves of Prophecy, but run
Clear from the very fountain of the Sun.
Ye call'd—and rightly call'd me—bloodhound; ye
That like old lagging dogs in self-despite
Must follow up the scent with me; with me,
Who having smelt the blood about this house
Already spilt, now bark of more to be.
For, though you hear them not, the infernal Choir

[260   ]

Whose dread antiphony forswears the lyre,

Who now are chaunting of that grim carouse

Of blood with which the children fed their Sire,

Shall never from their dreadful chorus stop

Till all be counter-pledged to the last drop.

CHORUS.

Hinting at what indeed has long been done,

And widely spoken, no Apollo needs; *(60)*

And for what else you aim at—still in dark

And mystic language—

CASSANDRA.

Nay, then, in the speech,

She that reproved me was so glib to teach—

Before yon Sun a hand's-breadth in the skies

He moves in shall have moved, those age-sick eyes

Shall open wide on Agamemnon slain

Before your very feet.   Now, speak I plain?

CHORUS.

Blasphemer, hush!

CASSANDRA.

Aye, hush the mouth you may,

But not the murder.

[261   ]

Chorus.

Murder! But the Gods—

(61)   ## Cassandra.

The Gods!
Who even now are their accomplices.

Chorus.

Woman! Accomplices—With whom?—

Cassandra.

With Her,
Who brandishing aloft the axe of doom,
    That just has laid one victim at her feet,
Looks round her for that other, without whom
    The banquet of revenge were incomplete.
Yet ere I fall will I prelude the strain
Of Triumph, that in full I shall repeat
When, looking from the twilight Underland,
I welcome Her as she descends amain,
Gash'd like myself, but by a dearer hand.
For that old murder'd Lion with me slain,
Rolling an awful eyeball through the gloom
He stalks about of Hades up to Day,
Shall rouse the whelp of exile far away,
(62) His only authentic offspring, ere the grim
Wolf crept between his Lioness and him;

Who with one stroke of Retribution, her

Who did the deed, and her adulterer,

Shall drive to hell; and then, himself pursued

By the wing'd Furies of his Mother's blood,

Shall drag about the yoke of Madness, till

Released, when Nemesis has gorged her fill,

By that same God, in whose prophetic ray

Viewing To-morrow mirror'd as To-day,

And that this House of Atreus the same wine

Themselves must drink they brew'd for me and mine;

I close my lips for ever with one prayer,

That the dark Warder of the World below

Would ope the portal at a single blow.

CHORUS.

And the raving voice, that rose

   Out of silence into speech

   Over-shooting human reach,

Back to silence foams and blows,

   Leaving all my bosom heaving—

Wrath and raving all, one knows;

Prophet-seeming, but if ever   *(63)*

   Of the Prophet-God possest,

   By the Prophet's self confest

God-abandon'd—woman's shrill

Anguish into tempest rising,
Louder as less listen'd.

                Still—

Spite of Reason, spite of Will,
What unwelcome, what unholy,
Vapour of Foreboding, slowly
Rising from the central soul's
Recesses, all in darkness rolls?
What! shall Age's torpid ashes
Kindle at the random spark
Of a raving maiden?—Hark!
What was that behind the wall?
A heavy blow—a groan—a fall—
Some one crying—Listen further—
Hark again then, crying "Murder!"
Some one—who then? Agamemnon?
Agamemnon?—Hark again!
Murder! murder! murder! murder!
Help within there! Help without there!
Break the doors in!—

(64)   CLYTEMNESTRA.

(Appearing from within, where lies AGAMEMNON *dead.)*[1]
                Spare your pain.
Look! I who but just now before you all

[1] *Hermann says, "Tractis tabulatis"—the scene* drawing—"*conspicitur Clytemnestra in conclavi stans ad corpus Agamemnonis.*"

Boasted of loyal wedlock unashamed,

Now unashamed dare boast the contrary.

Why, how else should one compass the defeat

Of him who underhand contrives one's own,

Unless by such a snare of circumstance

As, once enmesh'd, he never should break through?

The blow now struck was not the random blow

Of sudden passion, but with slow device

Prepared, and levell'd with the hand of time.

I say it who devised it; I who did;

And now stand here to face the consequence.

Ay, in a deadlier web than of that loom

In whose blood-purple he divined his doom,

And fear'd to walk upon, but walk'd at last,

Entangling him inextricably fast,

I smote him, and he bellow'd; and again

I smote, and with a groan his knees gave way;

And, as he fell before me, with a third   (65)

And last libation from the deadly mace

I pledged the crowning draught to Hades due,

The subterranean Saviour—of the Dead! [1]

At which he spouted up the Ghost in such

A burst of purple as, bespatter'd with,

No less did I rejoice than the green ear

[1] *At certain Ceremonies, the Third and crowning Libation was to Zeus Sotēr; and thus ironically to Pluto.*

[265   ]

Rejoices in the largess of the skies
That fleeting Iris follows as it flies.

CHORUS.

Oh woman, woman, woman!
By what accursèd root or weed
Of Earth, or Sea, or Hell, inflamed,
Darest stand before us unashamed
And, daring do, dare glory in the deed!

CLYTEMNESTRA.

Oh, I that dream'd the fall of Troy, as you
Belike of Troy's destroyer.   Dream or not,
Here lies your King—my Husband—Agamemnon,
Slain by this right hand's righteous handicraft.
(66) Like you, or like it not, alike to me;
To me alike whether or not you share
In making due libation over this
Great Sacrifice—if ever due, from him
Who, having charged so deep a bowl of blood,
Himself is forced to drink it to the dregs.

CHORUS.

Woman, what blood but that of Troy, which Zeus
Foredoom'd for expiation by his hand

For whom the penalty was pledged? And now,

Over his murder'd body, Thou

Talk of libation!—Thou! Thou! Thou!

But mark! Not thine of sacred wine

Over his head, but ours on thine

Of curse, and groan, and torn-up stone,

To slay or storm thee from the gate,

The City's curse, the People's hate,

Execrate, exterminate—

CLYTEMNESTRA.

Ay, ay, to me how lightly you adjudge

Exile or death, and never had a word

Of counter-condemnation for Him there; (67)

Who, when the field throve with the proper flock

For Sacrifice, forsooth let be the beast,

And with his own hand his own innocent

Blood, and the darling passion of my womb—

Her slew—to lull a peevish wind of Thrace.

And him who cursed the city with that crime

You hail with acclamation; but on me,

Who only do the work you should have done,

You turn the axe of condemnation. Well;

Threaten you me, I take the challenge up;

Here stand we face to face; win Thou the game,

And take the stake you aim at; but if I—

Then, by the Godhead that for me decides,
Another lesson you shall learn, though late.

CHORUS.

Man-mettled evermore, and now
Manslaughter-madden'd!   Shameless brow!
But do you think us deaf and blind
  Not to know, and long ago,
What Passion under all the prate
Of holy Justice made thee hate
Where Love was due, and love where—

(68)   ### CLYTEMNESTRA.

                    Nay, then, hear!
By this dead Husband, and the reconciled
Avenging Fury of my slaughter'd child,
I swear I will not reign the slave of fear
While he that holds me, as I hold him, dear,
Kindles his fire upon this hearth: my fast
Shield for the time to come, as of the past.
Yonder lies he that in the honey'd arms
Of his Chryseides under Troy walls
Dishonour'd mine: and this last laurell'd wench,
Prophetic messmate of the rower's bench,
Thus far in triumph his, with him along
Shall go, together chaunting one death-song,

[268   ]

To Hades—fitting garnish for the feast
Which Fate's avenging hand through mine hath drest.*

CHORUS.

Woe, woe, woe, woe!
That death as sudden as the blow
That laid Thee low would me lay low
Where low thou liest, my sovereign Lord!
Who ten years long to Trojan sword   (69)
Devoted, and to storm abroad,
 In one ill woman's cause accurst,
Liest slain before thy palace door
 By one accursedest and worst!

CLYTEMNESTRA.

Call not on Death, old man, that, call'd or no,
 Comes quick; nor spend your ebbing breath on me,
 Nor Helena: who but as arrows be
Shot by the hidden hand behind the bow.

CHORUS.

Alas, alas! The Curse I know
 That round the House of Atreus clings,
About the roof, about the walls,
 Shrouds it with his sable wings;

* " Has drest." (Edition of 1876.)

[269]

And still as each new victim falls,
And gorged with kingly gore,
Down on the bleeding carcase flings,
And croaks for "More, more, more!"

(70)   CLYTEMNESTRA.

Ay, now, indeed, you harp on likelier strings.
Not I, nor Helen, but that terrible
Alastor of old Tantalus in Hell;
Who, one sole actor in the scene begun
By him, and carried down from sire to son,
    The mask of Victim and Avenger shifts:
And, for a last catastrophe, that grim
    Guest of the abominable banquet lifts
His head from Hell, and in my person cries
For one full-grown sufficient sacrifice,
    Requital of the feast prepared for him
Of his own flesh and blood—And there it lies.

CHORUS.

Oh, Agamemnon! Oh, my Lord!
Who, after ten years toil'd;
After barbarian lance and sword
Encounter'd, fought, and foil'd;

Returning with the just award
Of Glory, thus inglorious by
Thine own domestic Altar die,
Fast in the spider meshes coil'd   *(71)*
Of Treason most abhorr'd!

CLYTEMNESTRA.

And by what retribution more complete,
Than, having in the meshes of deceit
Enticed my child, and slain her like a fawn
Upon the altar; to that altar drawn
Himself, like an unconscious beast, full-fed
With Conquest, and the garland on his head,
Is slain? and now, gone down among the Ghost,
Of taken Troy indeed may make the most,
But not *one* unrequited murder boast.

CHORUS.

Oh, Agamemnon, dead, dead, dead, dead, dead!
    What hand, what pious hand shall wash the wound
Through which the sacred spirit ebb'd and fled!
    With reverend care compose, and to the ground
Commit the mangled form of Majesty,
    And pour the due libation o'er the mound!

72

CLYTEMNESTRA.

This hand, that struck the guilty life away,
The guiltless carcase in the dust shall lay
With due solemnities: and if with no
Mock tears, or howling counterfeit of woe,
On this side earth; perhaps the innocent thing,
Whom with paternal love he sent before,
Meeting him by the melancholy shore,
Her arms about him with a kiss shall fling,
And lead him to his shadowy throne below.

CHORUS.

Alas! alas! the fatal rent
Which through the house of Atreus went,
Gapes again; a purple rain
Sweats the marble floor, and falls
From the tottering roof and walls,
The Dæmon heaving under; gone
The master-prop they rested on:
And the storm once more awake
　　Of Nemesis; of Nemesis
Whose fury who shall slake!

73

CLYTEMNESTRA.

Ev'n I; who by this last grand victim hope
The Pyramid of Vengeance so to cope,

That—and methinks I hear him in the deep
  Beneath us growling tow'rd his rest—the stern
  Alastor to some other roof may turn,
Leaving us here at last in peace to keep
What of life's harvest yet remains to reap.

CHORUS.

Thou to talk of reaping Peace
Who sowest Murder!   Woman, cease!
 And, despite that iron face—
Iron as the bloody mace
Thou bearest—boasting as if Vengeance
  Centred in that hand alone;
Know that, Fury pledg'd to Fury,
Vengeance owes himself the debts
He makes, and while he serves thee, whets
  His knife upon another stone,
Against thyself, and him with thee
Colleaguing, as you boast to be,
The tools of Fate.   But Fate is Zeus;
Zeus—who for awhile permitting   (74)
  Sin to prosper in his name,
Shall vindicate his own abuse;
And having brought his secret thought
  To light, shall break and fling to shame
The baser tools with which he wrought.

[273   ]

AGAMEMNON.

ÆGISTHUS: CLYTEMNESTRA: CHORUS.

All hail, thou daybreak of my just revenge!
In which, as waking from injurious sleep,
Methinks I recognize the Gods enthroned
In the bright conclave of eternal Justice,
Revindicate the wrongs of man to man!
For see *this* man—so dear to me now dead—
Caught in the very meshes of the snare
By which his father Atreus netted mine.
For that same Atreus surely, was it not?
Who, wrought by false Suspicion to fix'd Hate,[1]
From Argos out his younger brother drove,
My sire—Thyestes—drove him like a wolf,
Keeping his cubs—save one—to better purpose.
For when at last the home-heartbroken man
Crept humbly back again, craving no more
(75) Of his own country than to breathe its air
In liberty, and of her fruits as much
As not to starve withal—the savage King,
With damnable alacrity of hate,
And reconciliation of revenge,
Bade him, all smiles, to supper—such a supper,
Where the prime dainty was—my brother's flesh,

[1] *Or,*

> *Who, first suspecting falsely, and anon*
> *Detesting him his false suspicion wrong'd, &c.*

[274   ]

So maim'd and clipt of human likelihood,
That the unsuspecting* Father, light of heart,
And quick of appetite, at once fell to,
And ate—ate—what, with savage irony
As soon as eaten, told—the wretched man
Disgorging with a shriek, down to the ground
The table with its curst utensil dashed,
And, grinding into pieces with his heel,
Cried, loud enough for Heav'n and Hell to hear,
"Thus perish all the race of Pleisthenes!"
And now behold! the son of that same Atreus
By me the son of that Thyestes slain
Whom the kind brother, sparing from the cook,
Had with his victim pack'd to banishment;
Where Nemesis—(so sinners from some nook,
Whence least they think assailable, assailed)—
Rear'd me from infancy till fully grown,
To claim in full my father's bloody due.   (76)
Ay, I it was—none other—far away
Who spun the thread, which gathering day by day
Mesh after mesh, inch upon inch, at last
Reach'd him, and wound about him, as he lay,
And in the supper of his smoking Troy
Devour'd his own destruction—scarce condign
Return for that his Father forced on mine.

* Unspecting. (Edition of 1876.)

[275]

CHORUS.

Ægisthus, only things of baser breed
Insult the fallen; fall'n too, as you boast,
By one who plann'd but dared not do the deed.
This is your hour of triumph.   But take heed;
The blood of Atreus is not all outrun
With this slain King, but flowing in a son,
Who saved by such an exile as your own
For such a counter-retribution—

ÆGISTHUS.

Oh,
You then, the nether benchers of the realm,
Dare open tongue on those who rule the helm?
(77) Take heed yourselves; for, old and dull of wit,
And harden'd as your mouth against the bit,
Be wise in time; kick not against the spurs;
Remembering Princes are shrewd taskmasters.

CHORUS.

Beware thyself, bewaring me;
Remembering that, too sharply stirr'd,
The spurrer need beware the spurr'd;
As thou of me; whose single word

[276]

Shall rouse the City—yea, the very

   Stones you walk upon, in thunder

Gathering o'er your head, to bury

   Thee and thine Adultress under!

ÆGISTHUS.

   Raven, that with croaking jaws

      Unorphean, undivine,

   After you no City draws;

      And if any vengeance, mine

   Upon your wither'd shoulders—

CHORUS.   (78)

      Thine!

Who daring not to strike the blow

Thy worse than woman-craft design'd,

To worse than woman—

ÆGISTHUS.

    Soldiers, ho!

CLYTEMNESTRA.

Softly, good Ægisthus, softly; let the sword that has so

   deep

Drunk of righteous Retribution now within the scabbard

   sleep!

And if Nemesis be sated with the blood already spilt,

Even so let us, nor carry lawful Justice into Guilt.

Sheathe your sword; dismiss your spears; and you, Old
men, your howling cease,

And, ere ill blood come to running, each unto his home in
peace,

(79) Recognizing what is done for done indeed, as done it is,

And husbanding your scanty breath to pray that nothing
more amiss.

Farewell. Meanwhile, you and I, Ægisthus, shall de-
liberate,

When the storm is blowing under, how to settle House
and State.